> Gwen
> Thank you this writing project! Way more work than I'd ever dreamed. But all worth it if it helps those in need. God's blessing on you and Wendy too.
> His, Yours
> Tim & Kerri
> Eph 3:20,21

WHOLE-LY BROKEN

An inspirational memoir offering perspective and hope to chronic pain sufferers.

KERRI SHEPHERD

Copyright © 2023 Kerri Shepherd

All rights reserved. No portion of this book may be reproduced, stored in a retrieval system, or transmitted in any form or by any means — electronic, mechanical, photocopy, recording, scanning, or other — except for brief quotations in critical reviews or articles, without the prior written permission of the author.

Unless otherwise noted, Scripture is taken from the New International Version, copyright 1982, by Thomas Nelson. Used by permission. All rights reserved.

ISBN: 9798435892703

DEDICATION

This book is dedicated to my family.

My dear children, Jessica, Jonathan, and Julie,
in various ways the three of you have suffered
right along with me. From your early years,
you learned to serve me well, and you grew in grace
along with me in this trial. Through my illness,
I watched your character grow, so that now,
as adults, you all have such big hearts to serve others.
I have no greater joy than to know that
you and your children are walking in truth.
Jessica, Jonathan, and Julie, I am so proud of you.
You mean more to me than words could ever express.

And Tim, my faithful and loving husband,
you tirelessly encourage and help me in every possible way.
What could have destroyed our marriage,
brought us closer than I could have ever imagined.
By God's grace, we endure together.
Your strength gave me stability and security.
I cannot imagine a man of greater inner strength.
Words are insufficient to thank you for what your love,
encouragement, comfort, and faithfulness have meant to me.
Therefore, I will thank you with my life. I love you.
I am yours, and you are mine; but most importantly, we are His!

ACKNOWLEDGMENTS

There are so many people to thank who have played
an important role in my journey of suffering.
My memory would fail me to list all of you.
However, I would like to thank every single one of you
who have prayed for me in my illness and in the writing of this
book. I would not be here nor would this book without
that most important loving form of help.
I owe you a debt of gratitude.

Thanks to my nephew, Cory Hunter,
for his expertise in the cover design.

Thanks to Nichole Green, Gwen Ellis, and Bruce Enemark
for the hours they spent editing this manuscript.

Thanks to Rosie Cochran
for her proficiency in formatting this book.

Finally, thanks to the Health Care providers who for years stuck
with me and offered what help they could to rescue me from pain:
Vince Basile, Shari Berthold, Mona Chang, Kelly Douglas,
Todd Fausnaught, John Finkenstadt, Dwight Miller and Vicki Sims.

CONTENTS

	The Beginning	1
1	A New Normal	3
2	Provision in Agony	13
3	Desperate Times, Desperate Measures	26
4	You Can't Live Like This!	42
5	How Quickly Things Change	54
6	Déjà vu	64
7	So Close and Yet So Far	72
8	An Untamable Life of Its Own	91
9	Misery Loves Company	107
10	A Game Changer	114
11	Suffering Redeemed	124
12	Useless Pain	131
	In Conclusion	145
	Appendix	146
	Endnotes	151
	About the Author	156

The Beginning

What if you woke up tomorrow and could no longer do whatever you usually do in life? What if you lost everything you owned and had no insurance policy to replace a dime of it? What if you lost the use of your limbs or your emotional stability? If a tsunami-sized trial hit your life, what would hold *you* when you could no longer hold on? Would your identity be secure, and your life still have meaning?

We don't have to look far to find such victims of personal tragedies: they're everywhere. No doubt, you've had family or friends experience profound or ongoing suffering. Perhaps you are the sufferer and feel so alone. If so, I'd like to pull up a chair alongside of you and let you know that you're not alone.

As you read from these pages of my life, these chapters that I never signed up for, you'll see how such an insecure situation made me a more secure person filled with meaning and purpose despite severe disability, massive frustration, and pain. Discover how vulnerable situations taught me valuable lessons. Learn how our significance doesn't have to be rooted in temporal things. This is how it all began.

* * *

It was one of those popsicle-sticky summer Saturdays in the early 1970s. As playground swings squeaked and balls bounced, Claire and

I joined the gang of kids headed to the seesaw. Our group divided as we piled onto both sides of the seesaw. Unfortunately, I was on the very end of one side when all the kids on the other side carelessly jumped off. That hard, dusty ground offered no protection. And never again would I be naïve of the dangers of a simple seesaw.

For the next hour, I lay there in pain, waiting for my friend to walk back to her house to call my parents. That split-second decision of those children, to jump off their end, undoubtedly played a significant role in the decades of my debilitating pain. How could that possibly be? Let me explain.

CHAPTER 1
A New Normal
1991-1993

I was twenty-seven years old and living in the small frontier town of Puerto Ayacucho in the Amazon territory of Venezuela when my debacle began. This primitive town had one traffic light when we moved there. It was the last stop before the pristine jungle. Tim and I had been married for seven years and had moved with our baby girl to Venezuela four years prior. We belonged to a mission organization and worked alongside a team of others serving various ethnic groups tucked away in the Amazon jungle. I had given birth to two more children during those four years.

The end of what I would have considered a normal, healthy, fulfilling life began the day I finally responded to my need to lose the 10-15 pounds I'd gained from my recent pregnancy. I started back into my aerobic exercise routine, one that I had done for years. At the end of my workout, back spasms began and took over my life!

Dirty diapers are as common to babies as backaches are to young moms, especially given how we lug them around from one hip to the other. I had had episodes of back pain in the past, but they typically never lasted more than a few hours or a couple of days. However, what began to unravel that day was unlike anything I could've imagined. As the weeks went by, my injury refused to heal. My whole life revolved around this pain. Frustration mounted as I struggled through each day trying to care for our little ones. What was generating this pain? Why wouldn't it stop?

I let several weeks pass before seeing a local doctor. Because of the stories I had heard, I had little confidence in the medical help available in town. Besides, in my growing-up years, I'd heard my dad say over and over that "these kinds of things work themselves out."

In our Amazonian podunk town, you didn't need an appointment to see the doctor. Instead, you would just show up at the doctor's office, sign in, and then stand or sit in the dirt courtyard waiting for your turn, which may or may not be in the order that you arrived. I couldn't stand, and I could only sit for a few minutes. When I finally did see the doctor, he gave me the typical medication cocktail for back pain: a muscle relaxant, an anti-inflammatory, and pain medication. He told me to stay in bed for two weeks.

I followed the doctor's orders but was none the better for it. I had minimal time every day to function normally before debilitating back spasms would take over. On average, I could be on my feet for approximately a quarter of every hour. If I overextended my uptime, I would have to lie down much longer to recover. If I was up a lot in the morning, I would have to be down the rest of the day. If I wanted to do something in the evening, I would have to lie down all day so that I could go out. The longer I rested, the longer I could be up and about.

Weight-bearing positions such as standing or sitting were the worst! That meant that I was usually lying on my side in the fetal position on the living room floor. Because wearing my glasses in that position was so uncomfortable, I quit wearing them.

Sometimes I'd brush my teeth in the shower while getting wet in order to cut down on standing time. I longed for a bathtub, but they didn't sell them in our town. Sometimes I'd squeeze into the kid's little blue plastic tub, and let my legs hang over the edge, just so I didn't have to stand to shower. Even raising my arms to wash my hair increased the pain. It was a good thing I had short hair.

I remember one morning being in tears from the pain as I stood waiting for the last pancake to cook, when it dawned on me that I wasn't wearing my elastic back brace. For crying out loud, muscles are supposed to heal! Why weren't mine healing? This situation was perplexing and discouraging. I was caring for three children under the age of five; no momma has time for this!

As the months of relentless low back spasms rolled by, Tim and I realized that my monthly cycle was a significant factor. It put me completely down for about ten days every month. I tried hard not to aggravate my back, but there was nothing I could do about that aspect.

If you've had severe back issues, you know that even when you do nothing all day, you still use your back muscles. The body's natural functions like coughing, sneezing, laughing, crying, and even defecation, can bump up your level of pain. You can only imagine my fear when those around me got a stomach bug. Life seemed to be one step forward and two steps backward. No wonder it felt like a losing battle. I can't think of a single area of my life that this problem didn't affect.

Back spasms became a "pain dictator" that brought much unwelcomed change. To-do lists and schedules became a thing of the past. My idea of essentials was continually shrinking as I learned to cut corners and even avoid them. We had to make some necessary changes around the house. Julie, our ten-month-old, shared a room with our three-year-old Jonathan. She had to be moved from her crib to a toddler bed, as this was much safer than having Jessica, her five-year-old sister, lift her in and out of the crib when Tim wasn't home. We replaced our waterbed with a firm mattress. Things I needed from the upper cupboards were moved to the countertops because reaching increased my pain. My social life was scaled way back. People who came to visit got their own drinks. If they were really good friends, they lifted a hand to do whatever undone chore stood out to them.

Convenience foods did not exist in the grocery stores of our town. Meals were made from scratch except for bread and the corn flakes we ate on Sunday mornings. I used our crockpot for very simple meals. The worse I felt, the less I could keep our home or myself the way I wanted.

Cleaning became less important to me. As a family, we pulled together to make up for my deficit. Once I remember peering into Jonathan's bedroom to see him sitting on the floor, feeding little pieces of lint and dirt into the vacuum's hose. The machine was just too big and bulky for him to push around on his area rug. While it was very cute, it made me feel sad.

Sometimes I needed the older two kids to go outside to hang out the laundry. Jessica would stand on a chair to reach the clothesline while Jonathan would hand her one item at a time. I can still picture Jonathan dodging fire ants at his feet while clean diapers blew in the wind over their little blond heads in that hot tropical sun.

You've heard that "play is the work of childhood." Well, my kids turned work into play. I often saw their work become big-time fun! Our kids often laughed, splashed, and got soaked while washing the supper dishes. Living in that sweltering climate, our clothes and waxed cement floors throughout the house dried in no time. During the dry season, the wind blew in a light film of dust, which covered the open-louvered glass windowpanes and floors. When Jessica mopped up that dust from the floors with a wet towel thrown over a squeegee, 'slip n slide' was soon to occur. There was a bit of a slant to the floor, so she and Jonathan would just open up the front door, slide down the hallway, and right out onto the front porch. I'd put some water in the tray of little Julie's walker so she wouldn't miss out on the wet fun! I'm not sure how much of their help they perceived as work. But this was our new norm, and I was proud of them for picking up the slack. Eventually, we hired someone to come twice a week to do housework.

For me, the pain was a breeding ground for guilt. It made me sad that I couldn't play with Julie the way I had played with the other kids at that early stage of their lives. I couldn't bear her body weight, much less my own. I tried to comfort myself with the fact that I was always on the floor, available to her. But I felt guilty lying on the floor three-fourths of the day. It was hard to balance the needs of the kids with my own needs.

I felt guilty for doing the dishes and guilty for not doing them. I remember Tim arriving home from work and getting ticked at me struggling in pain just to stand up in front of a sink chock-full of dishes. Yet, when I explained that I just needed the baby's bottle from somewhere under that pile, he understood.

I felt guilty for Tim's increased workload at home. I was no longer the capable woman he had married. I felt guilty that I could not help my co-workers as I used to, since I could barely keep my home afloat. I felt guilty that during my flare-ups, I needed their help.

Down the road, I felt guilty for all the financial burdens this caused. On and on went my guilt. It may seem illogical to feel guilty for something you couldn't control, but I didn't know how to stop that feeling.

I was a "go-getter" type and loved physical work. From childhood, I repeatedly heard my mom say that it was "a good day if you got a lot done." By that definition, I'd had many "good days" before debilitating pain took over my life. Tim used to say that my list for the day should have been for the week. Life had been busy before, but not overwhelming. Now, everything had changed. How was I to measure a good day now? Were my good days over? What could I possibly accomplish on the floor? I wanted my life to have meaning and purpose, but the oppressive pain was driving me toward insignificance. It was as if God had pulled me out of the game of life and "benched" me. I called this "shelf life" because I felt like I had been placed on a shelf, up and out of the way of life.

Once our next-door neighbors had their elderly parents come from the USA for a visit. I watched from my window as this adorable couple put forth a serious effort to climb the set of stairs up to the front door. When it dawned on me that I was empathizing with them, it gave me pause. If I am identifying with this elderly couple now, while I'm in my twenties, what will I feel like in another decade or two, let alone if I got anywhere near their age? At that moment fear gripped my heart, just imagining how hard life could get as I aged. I had to get this pain resolved! But where would we get the money to do so? Could we possibly take a medical leave of absence?

Tim bought supplies for approximately fifty families that lived deep in the middle of the jungle. Those fifty families worked among various indigenous people groups that call Venezuela home. Each people group had its own distinct culture and language. It was not uncommon in those days to see people from a few of these ethnic groups in our frontier town, sometimes wearing nothing more than a loincloth. These families, living far from any grocery store (or any store for that matter), depended on Tim's service to remain at their stations; it would be too expensive and too time-consuming for them to secure supplies for themselves.

I had lived with relentless pain for ten months before we flew to the capital city of Caracas to look for help. Our family traveled there in conjunction with a necessary trip out of the country to renew our visas. With peanut butter, jelly, and bread in our suitcases, we made the short jaunt from the international airport on the northern coast of Venezuela to Curaçao for a night and then returned to Venezuela. I can't remember from that trip what doctor(s) I saw in Caracas or what imaging I had done at that point. But I do remember two things: traveling was very painful, and the doctor(s) saw nothing wrong. Certainly, someone should've seen something wrong with me; I wasn't making this up!

I used to imagine myself lying on the floor of my hometown library back in the States, pouring over piles of medical books, trying to figure out for myself what was wrong. (Obviously, these were pre-internet days.) This monster was all-consuming: there wasn't an aspect of my life that this growing problem didn't touch! Pain, my worst enemy, yet closest companion, was ruining my otherwise happy life.

Honestly, after now living with this condition for two years, I'd lost my desire to live. There were many days when I thought the most merciful thing God could do would be to take me in a car crash. That way, my family could then have a better wife and mom, not this broken one wracked by pain and perpetual bed head.

Not having the privilege of knowing what was wrong with me was very hard. I didn't have answers to everyone's questions, much less my own. Though I know people asked about my condition out of love and concern, their asking created unwanted pressure. Because no one could relate to what I was going through, it was lonely and scary. I often ran dry on the courage needed to deal with this relentless pain and discouragement, but I tried not to let it show.

Because of my poor physical condition, I reasoned that it was all the more important to be intact in the other areas of my life. I tried very hard not to let what was happening to me physically affect me emotionally, mentally, or spiritually. I didn't allow myself to cry. I reasoned that caving into self-pity would be my undoing.

Schooling my young ones was a positive mental distraction that I could do while lying on the floor. Though their young ages meant great responsibility, their cute antics peppered my days with much-needed laughter! Their constant physical, emotional, mental, and spiritual needs helped me to peel my eyes off my struggles. You only get one crack at parenting, and with all my heart, I wanted to do it right! It grieved me when I could not care for my family the way that I wanted, the way that I thought they needed to be cared for.

Could all this suffering have a worthy purpose? Before these initial years of chronic pain, I would have answered, "Yes." I believed the biblical teaching that God uses everything that happens to us for our good and His glory if we allow Him to. The Bible teaches that one reason God allows His children to suffer so is that they can help others in their suffering; then we can empathize.

After two years of constant pain and major limitations, I wore down and confessed to God that I was just too selfish and didn't care if I ever got to help someone else that was suffering. I'd fought to believe that this pain could be redeemed. I wanted out! Subtly, I began my pilgrimage of nagging doubt. What good for me or others could possibly be eked out of all this suffering? It was a big waste of my days! This battle grew more intense as time marched on.

Whether physical or emotional, chronic pain of any nature has a way of draining the happiness out of your life and making you more self-absorbed. Pain is meant to be a warning signal, not a parasite sucking the life out of you. It's bitter, evil, and exhausting! I found it a real struggle not to give in to despondency.

One day Tim came home with a book for me called *Laugh Again: Experience Outrageous Joy* by Chuck Swindoll. I initially took offense at my husband's kindness. It wasn't long, however, before I began to appreciate the author's motto to "set your sails for joy no matter what your circumstances."[1] Quite challenging! This book walked me through the ancient yet relevant New Testament book of Philippians. Its message was scribed by the revolutionary apostle Paul when he, at the pinnacle of his successful career, was put under house arrest and chained to a Roman guard. He knew a thing or two about confinement. Under these circumstances, Paul writes about joy to the first century persecuted followers of Jesus. That study was the catalyst for change in my attitude toward suffering as I determined to make the best of my situation and not succumb to bitterness.

Mover and shaker Helen Keller, both blind and deaf, said, "I am grateful for my handicap, for, through it, I have found my world, myself, and my God."[2] She couldn't control her circumstances, but she could control her attitude toward them. This author, lecturer, activist, and American legend also said, "So much has been given to me I have not time to ponder over that which has been denied."[3]

Having earnestly asked God for healing over those last two years, I sensed a need to change the direction of my prayers. Rather than strictly begging for a "light at the end of the tunnel," I asked God to help me see what gems of truth He had for me to learn inside this dark cavern of pain. Precious gems of this earth are not basking in the sunlight on sidewalks for just any passerby to snatch up. No, they lie in its darkest caves. I was about to take up spiritual spelunking, without even leaving my bed, to search for gems of truth in the dark crevices of my debilitation.

A year later, I flew back up to Caracas, the country's capital, for a week of testing with the hope of finding answers. I was passed from an orthopedic doctor to a nephrologist and then to a neurologist and on to a doctor of internal medicine. I had the standard battery of testing required from each specialist. Each of them agreed I was in great shape; no pain source was found.

The last specialist I saw was either a psychologist or a psychiatrist; I can't remember. He concluded that all my dysfunction was a result of stress, so he put me on Valium. You can only imagine my frustration at that point! If one of the doctors had said, "You have cancer and only a few months to live," I would have a diagnosis, drugs for pain, and an end in sight! I'm sorry; that sounds very insensitive to individuals dealing with cancer, but those were my raw thoughts. I was no closer to a solution than I was at the beginning of the week. Only now, I felt closer to hopelessness. I concurred with the Solomonic proverb, that "hope deferred makes the heart sick."

Back home, I asked some of my friends for an objective opinion: Did they think all of this could come from stress? Their unanimous conclusion was that it was the pain that was adding the stress, not the other way around. Tim and I have a rather laid-back nature. Apart from this pain, I had a wonderful life!

Why does nothing show up when something is very obviously wrong? I remember bemoaning my plight before God one night: "Are you just pressing a thumb into my back so I hurt? No! No! You wouldn't do that. Would You?" My lack of healing did not come from a lack of asking or from a lack of faith. I didn't doubt that the God who created everything could hear me and heal me.

My brother and sister-in-law, who knew nothing of our medical bills from that week, gave us an extra-large sum of money that same week, that "just happened" to equal the sum of all those medical bills. It boosted my faith to see God provide like that for us financially, especially because we had no financial reserve!

Another great timely help was a friend's recommendation to take daily vitamin B shots since they help our bodies deal with stress. With the Valium and vitamin B injections, I was able to sit up comfortably for an hour, rather than my typical maximum of 15 minutes.

What a timely help, as our scheduled "leave and reprieve" visit back to our home country for a year was quickly approaching.

A Closer Look at the DESIGNER

Profound suffering changes us; we choose to become bitter or better. In times of fiery trial, some choose to run to God, some run away from Him, and others say they just don't believe in His existence.

Common sense tells me that anytime there is a design, there is a designer. Every kid knows that when you shake a bucket of Lego bricks, they won't self-construct. Those little bricks would be reduced to powder before that would happen.

But how can we trust someone we don't know? From the vast galaxies to the tiniest laminin adhesion protein in the bedrock of our cells, and everything in between, everything reveals something of our Divine Architect's nature! This full-of-wonder world proclaims His utter intelligence, immaculate forethought, inexhaustible creativity, scrupulous care, exquisite beauty, impeccable design, and infinite power! Wow! It means so much to me that God didn't make me because He needed me, but because He wanted me!

I find that getting to know God more helps me move from bitter thinking to better thinking. Someone wisely said, "Removing God from the picture doesn't remove or diminish our suffering; it eliminates our ability to navigate through it successfully."

How can I understand who I am and why I am here unless I understand the nature of my Designer and the value that He places on me? Not knowing God or keeping my distance from Him results in idolatry — creating "gods" of my own making. But understanding and rehearsing God's character, as revealed in the Bible, has had a profound impact on my suffering, helping to quiet the angst of my future, my unanswered questions, and my fears.

The better I know Him (not just knowing about Him, but personally knowing Him), the more I trust Him. Because God designed me and can fix every broken part of me, I have hope that in His time and in His way, He will!

"When you and I hurt deeply, what we really need is not an explanation from God but a revelation of God. We need to see how great God is; we need to recover our lost perspective on life. Things get out of proportion when we are suffering, and it takes a vision of something bigger than ourselves to get life's dimensions adjusted again."[4] — Warren W. Wiersbe

CHAPTER 2

Provision in Agony
1991-1996

In August 1993, we boarded a plane in Caracas, Venezuela, and flew back to the USA. My daughter Julie and I had an empty seat in our row. As the plane filled up, everyone passed by our row of seats. Once they shut the doors to the plane, I was shocked to look around and see that the only empty seat was the one in our row. I was so relieved because now I could lie on the floor in front of our seats. Otherwise, I didn't know how I would have been able to sit up for the five-hour flight. Divine Providence!

After being gone for four years, it was great being back home with family, friends, and all things familiar. Back to the land of bathtubs, strawberries, and department stores! We spent the first couple of weeks in America visiting my family in Pennsylvania. Right away people noticed that I had gotten quite thin. I'd heard through the grapevine that some people thought I was anorexic. The pain had subtly affected my appetite as well as my ability to sit at the table for the normal duration of a meal, although I made myself eat as much as Julie (now three years old).

No one back home knew how much the pain had affected me, as it was never the main topic of my letters. And once we left Venezuela, I lost access to injectable vitamin B shots. When I started taking the equivalent over-the-counter synthetic B vitamins, food didn't taste good, not even my favorite foods that I'd been looking forward to eating for the last four years.

Living with chronic pain can be much like hearing static noise on the radio. It's very annoying and can make it difficult to perceive and relate to the things going on around you. When pain is your very closest companion, you try as hard as you can to push through it in order to make whatever you can of your life. But sadly, in some cases, you can no longer negotiate with your pain.

Now that we were in the USA with a whole year to pursue answers, I was again hopeful. We made the 500-mile trip to visit our dear Kentucky family; I had a sliver of a spot on the floor of the van where I could lie down.

While in Kentucky, I paid a visit to a doctor who was recommended to me. He immediately took me off the Valium that I had started taking back in Venezuela, which was a very smart move but quite unpleasant. Valium is a great drug, but very addictive and not good for long-term use. Thankfully, it helped me make it through all the traveling and a much-needed root canal that I wouldn't have been able to sit up for. Because I had been on Valium for a few months, I went through some withdrawal. Unfortunately, the newly prescribed medication did absolutely nothing to help me; in fact, it had an adverse effect on me. When I couldn't mentally keep track of my medications or cope with the kids, Tim became frustrated with me. I remember telling him to treat me like a child, if needed.

After our time in Kentucky, we settled into an apartment in Pennsylvania. As soon as possible, I made an appointment with a recommended local chiropractor named Dwight. It was obvious to him that some, if not all, of my pain was coming from the sacroiliac (SI) joint. I never took anatomy in high school, so I didn't even know I had one — or two as is the case.

At the base of the spine is a triangular-shaped bone called the sacrum. Where your sacrum meets your left and right ilium (the large butt bones) are two sacroiliac joints. They are unlike any other joint in the body. They are covered by two different kinds of cartilage. The sacrum is covered with a layer of hyaline (glassy and slick) and the ilium is covered with dense fibrocartilage. These rub against each other with underlying, coarse-textured bones with depressions and ridges that provide great friction. They are designed to give stability to the whole body as it transmits all the forces of the upper body to the pelvis and legs. These joints are designed for very little movement, only about 2-4 millimeters.

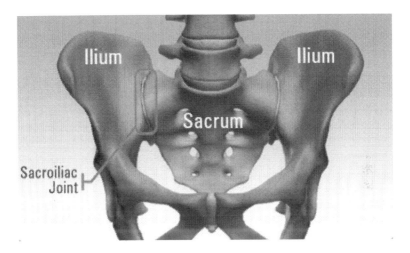

The Human Pelvis[5]

My muscles in that whole area were so hard that Dwight couldn't manipulate the bones into proper alignment, but he was able to make some change. The muscles were making a valiant effort to provide pelvic stability but compensating for loose ligaments was not their God-given role. It amazes me to see how well the body works together to care for its weaknesses and abnormalities. Until I better understood the mechanics of this joint, I would get so confused. One week I would hear that the joint was locked and the next week that it was hypermobile. Both were actually true.

On the day of my first chiropractic adjustment, I started having bowel cramping and diarrhea, which became rather violent and lasted for days! All of this abdominal cramping and diarrhea was really aggravating my back; I was miserable! The arrangement of our less-than-ideal apartment for those six months required me to go down two flights of stairs to use the bathroom and to crawl back up. It wasn't long before we got a portable toilet for our bedroom. Emptying that nasty thing was just one of the hundreds of ways my sweet husband demonstrated his unconditional love for me!

When I saw Dwight the following week, he asked if I was feeling any better, and I had to tell him that I was worse. I happened to mention that I was about ready to start a treatment for some unwelcome parasites that I thought had hitched a ride back with me from the tropics. He asked me when those symptoms started. When I told him that it was shortly after my treatment, he seemed to think that the abdominal pain and reactive bowel was connected to his attempt to align me. Soon we saw a definite pattern connecting the two. The first three months of chiropractic treatments were miserable! I had my doubts that the adjustments were even worth it. I didn't want to eat, knowing that shortly afterward severe cramping would follow, so I snacked lightly. Then finally those nasty bowel episodes tapered off and came to a blessed stop. I started functioning and enjoying food again! I was about 25 pounds under my recommended weight.

Before moving to Kentucky for the second half of our furlough, Dwight showed Tim how to adjust my sacroiliac joint. My right ilium was always wedged upward, and my sacrum was usually a bit rotated. Not long after we moved, Tim started having trouble adjusting me the way the chiropractor had shown him. Because he wasn't getting things aligned properly, the chronic pain and dysfunction returned. So, Tim developed his own primitive yet effective method. He would place his flattened left hand over the top crest of my right ilium, make a fist with his right hand, and pound downward. Eventually, he pounded on a flip-flop instead of his hand.

It worked! As long as I was aligned, I felt good! The challenge was to get the joint to hold its proper position. Everywhere we went, I constantly needed to get aligned. If I didn't get aligned, a muscle spasm would escalate. We tried to be as discreet as possible when we were in public. Not just because it was embarrassing, but also because Tim had to pound so hard; I was so afraid that someone would see us and get the wrong idea.

In those months I made some special memories doing normal mom things like playdates, picnics, parks, and library visits.

When our time in America came to a close, I felt more and more uneasy about returning to Venezuela. We had a better understanding of my pain and seemingly a way to manage it, but in my opinion, my back issue was far from resolved! But we didn't know how we could've stayed longer on a medical leave without a medical diagnosis. Where else could we go to find a diagnosis? The answer to that question was many years and tears down the road.

Upon returning to our home in Venezuela, I began to hang from my knees for structural alignment. The mango tree in our backyard was my "hanging tree" and Jessica, Jonathan, and Julie's favorite climbing tree. It had an easily accessible branch that Tim helped me on and off of, while one of the kids kept our adorable boxers, Buster and Babes, from smothering my face with kisses! We had not yet heard of inversion tables, but this was our idea of using gravity to pull that joint into place with my body's weight. We figured it would be better for my sacroiliac joint than the constant pounding. Sometimes I could feel or hear the joint pop into place; other times the muscles in that area were so contracted that nothing budged. There were also days when my sinuses wouldn't allow that kind of pressure to my head. On those days Tim would resort to pounding on the joint. I would hang from the mango tree a couple of times a week or a couple of times a day, depending on the need. My pain always told me when it was time to hang. I was never pain-free for long, but thankfully, now I had periods of relief!

Over the next two years, I bounced in and out of flare-ups. We were still able to make some good family memories with our kids. We were able to visit three different isolated tribal bases where our organization worked. We loved Saturdays when we could drive to one of the tributaries of the Orinoco River and escape the tropical heat in the cool, refreshing water. Tobogan de la Selva, a huge natural rock waterslide only a half an hour away, became a favorite of our children as they got older.

I was thankful for the diversion of homeschooling our two oldest children. I enjoyed it, and it gave me something other than my pain to focus on. In light of needing to put school on hold for several weeks at a time when I got into back flare-ups, someone pointed out what a huge blessing it was that our kids were such quick learners. This was something that I had completely taken for granted.

I remember one flare-up in particular on Jessica's ninth birthday. Unable to have our typical birthday parties, I was only able to allow her to invite two friends over. They played some table games and dipped bananas in some melted chocolate chips for a special treat. She didn't seem to care that I couldn't be up long enough to make her a cake. I certainly couldn't do all that I wanted to do for my kids, but I consoled myself in the fact that I was always available to them.

By now, I had completely stopped bending over because of the pain it inflicted. I was rather adept at picking up things off the floor with my toes. I got a kick out of watching the kids try to copy me. It was a good reminder that they were constantly observing all my attitudes and reactions toward pain and limitation. I continued to work at "setting my sails for joy," as Chuck Swindoll's book said to do — to make the best of my circumstances, to look on the bright side, and to see my cup as half full. But the tentacles of negativity constantly threatened to strangle me. There was no way to avoid these flare-ups since I didn't know what was going to cause them. It was always something different that would cause my back to flare up. Things that I could do safely one day would cause me to pay dearly the next; my boundaries were constantly moving. It's not like I was painting or moving furniture. Just "normal" life, doing nothing out of the ordinary, threw me into a tailspin. Why that joint wouldn't stay in place gnawed at me, but I didn't know what to do about it.

In January of 1996, I developed an issue that required seeing a gynecologist in Caracas. This doctor seemed very interested in my overall health and asked me a ton of questions. After learning of my chronic pain and my need for constant alignment, she wondered why no one recommended fusing the sacroiliac joint. She gave me the name of a colleague, whom I'd learned was considered to be the top orthopedic surgeon in all of South America.

When I got home, I talked things over with Tim. Several weeks later, I returned to Caracas with Julie for a consultation with Dr. Uzcategui, the recommended orthopedic. He ordered several tests: more x-rays, another MRI, a bone scan, and even a three-dimensional CT image of my pelvis, which was state of the art at the time. The crazy thing was, I felt unusually well for these tests. It made getting to and from the hospital so much easier, which was great! (Getting around in a city of two million people can be a challenge even when you have your health.) But now I was afraid that the tests wouldn't reveal the abnormality because my sacroiliac (SI) joint was holding its proper position. I thought that for them to see what was wrong, they needed to see my SI joint misaligned. Therefore, I decided to carry Julie, who had just turned five years old, to a nearby park to play. I hoped that that would work to my benefit, but it did not. I had so much to learn about my condition.

After all my testing, the doctor said I had a herniated disc between L4 and L5 and mentioned that my SI joint looked like that of a 70-year-old. He put me on a new combination of medication and told me to come back when I could no longer live with it. I had reached that point three years ago! When I began to quietly cry, he asked my friend, Susan, who accompanied me to my doctor's appointment, if I was depressed. *Desperate was more like it!*

The disc wasn't the problem. I had no sharp shooting or burning nerve pain and no pain in my SI joint either. I had severe muscle spasms in the lower lumbar region which caused debilitating pain. One needy part of the body does not like to suffer alone. When I couldn't get the back spasms to calm down in good time, spasms in my neck and headaches soon came to join the pain party. When things really got out of hand, my muscles that wrap around to my front ribs would spasm and pull my vertebra out of alignment. Then my digestive system would complain.

Sure enough, the week of doctor's appointments, tests, and carrying Julie to the park all caught up with me the night before our flight back home. Sadly, Tim wasn't there to align my SI joint. By the time we got home, I couldn't unpack, shower, or do anything but lie on the floor in the fetal position with ice packs. The next two days held the worst pain I had experienced yet. I couldn't tolerate being touched to be aligned, and I got very weak from the severe pain.

On the third day my pain was out of control, and I became unglued emotionally. I desperately needed help! I couldn't take care of my kids, and they were too young to take care of me.

Thankfully, we had gotten a telephone line about six months prior. After living at this residence for eight years, we had finally received a phone number. (The territory we were living in at the time only had so many phone numbers, so you had to wait until one became available.) Jonathan, now seven years old, got on the phone and started calling around for his dad's whereabouts. He wasn't able to talk with Tim, as he was out in the town buying supplies that day. But he did get my dear friend Michele on the line (who 14 years later became his mother-in-law). Michele dropped everything and came to our rescue. She not only tended to me and the kids, but she also continued trying to track down Tim. Michele was able to get ahold of our co-worker Susie, who was a nurse. She and Susie began searching our little town for medication for extreme pain. The strongest medication they located was Demerol. The clinic said they only had one dose of it. They also tried to track down Dr. Uzcategui in Caracas.

Late in the day, our dear friends, Howard and Susan, who lived in Caracas, were able to get ahold of Dr. Uzcategui. After explaining my predicament, he prescribed ten injections of Nubian which they picked up for me. Howard and Susan passed those injections to another co-worker of ours who was flying down to our town the next morning. What a blessing it was to have these friends going above and beyond to try to get me the help I needed. Tim and I were praying that these shots would put me back on the road to recovery.

The next day, after receiving the medication, Tim was shocked to see that it barely took the edge off of my pain.

As the tropical sun poured through our bedroom window the following morning, I looked over at my waking husband and said to him, "You have to get me out of here." And I was thinking, *because if you don't, I'm not going to make it.* I was weak, scared, and in a tremendous amount of severe pain! I was at the end of my ability to cope. News about my condition must have spread quickly because a co-worker pilot had already flown a Cessna plane out from the interior late in the afternoon of the previous day, not the next morning as was originally planned. I guess there was suspicion that we might need an emergency flight up to Caracas. They were right!

Later that day, I was carried out of the house and laid carefully in the back of someone's vehicle. Jessica, whose tenth birthday was just around the corner, had packed a couple of suitcases for all of us. We had no idea then, but that day we were leaving our home of eight years and never coming back. There were no good-byes to our friends, co-workers, and two boxers, who had just the month before given us their second litter of adorable pups. A seat was removed in the Cessna so that I could lie flat for the three-hour flight to Caracas. The turbulence made things all the more agonizing. But I hoped my destination would bring relief.

What a huge disappointment. The military airport where we landed was still an hour's drive from the hospital. After learning that, I remember thinking: *I may as well just lie here and die.* As unreasonable as that may sound, that's what was going through my head. That was until I looked up and saw my Julie, Jonathan, and Jessica looking down at me, their eyes pleading that I would be okay. No ambulance awaited me, but Howard was there with his compact car to drive us to the hospital. His wife Susan was going to meet us there. I was asked if I wanted to wait for an ambulance, which would have been dispatched from a location an hour away. I felt like I couldn't wait that long, but nor could I imagine sitting up in a car for an hour. I asked if there was ice available. Since there was, I told them to pack my back in ice for the car ride. The pressure from sitting up, jarring from potholes, and the turns in the road made for a horrendous trip. In retrospect, I wish I had waited for the ambulance.

Just as the Policlinica Metropolitana Hospital came into view, I began to shake uncontrollably. I was told that my lips were blue. I suppose I'll never know if it was from shock or from all that ice.

Jessica remembers that day well; too well, my poor darling. "Mom, you looked like death to my ten-year-old eyes. I saw you shaking and bluish. I thought you were gone. That day, when I packed our suitcases, ended my childhood." It was definitely a pivotal day in her life.

I was wheeled into the emergency room on a stretcher and taken directly to a private cubical, where I waited and waited and waited. *Why is no one coming? When am I going to get something for this pain?*

I was beyond upset that I had traveled so far and was so bad off and still wasn't getting any help. This top-notch hospital that held out so much hope for my dire circumstances offered me nothing. How inconvenient could a shot of morphine have been?

Screaming may have helped, but I couldn't vocalize anything. I was so weak that I could barely whisper. I remember focusing in on my husband and in barely a whisper, I pushed out the words, "I'm sorry."

I wanted to tell him that I was sorry to leave him to raise our three kids on his own. It had always been our little joke that if something happened to me, Tim was going to place an ad in the *Moody Monthly* magazine, "Desperate father of three in need of a wife!"

The extent of God's love became clear to me when I was in that emergency room in Caracas, Venezuela. I remember praying rather piecemeal thoughts.

> *I'm in agony; Jesus, You know agony. I'm extremely weak; You know extreme weakness. ... I can't get out of this. ... Oh God! See me. Help me! ... Every second of Your crucifixion, You chose to be there. ... You could've escaped. ... I can't! But I would if I had a choice. ... Why didn't You? ... Your pain was excruciating! ... You didn't escape because You loved me. ... WOW! Oh, Abba! What love! Love kept You there. ... I better understand Your love for me now. ... How You love me! ... I will go to You because You suffered for me. ... I can't. ... So weak. ... I'm Yours.*

I learned that there were heart attack victims on either side of me in the Emergency Room. I prayed for the one on my right and the other on my left as I drifted in and out consciousness. I was thinking about Jesus, of course. I had a better idea of what agony was now. But I fell way short of the anguish Jesus suffered on that Roman cross. No one can fathom the depth of His suffering, as it ran way deeper than the physical. No human will ever understand the torment of Jesus being forsaken by His Father while bearing the sin of the world.

The white coats finally came in to see me and gave me some medication. For my "side order" of suffering — not being able to urinate — they gave me a catheter. More x-rays were taken to ensure nothing had changed in the week since I had last seen my doctor.

While they were taking the x-rays, I remember thinking: *These x-rays are worthless; they'll show nothing! This is one crazy story. Who would believe that you could be in this much pain, yet have "nothing wrong" with you?* If I wasn't in so much pain, it could've been embarrassing.

Howard and Susan cared for our three children plus their own two kids in their tiny apartment while we spent the next three weeks in the hospital. It wasn't like me to not think about or even ask about my children, but the pain inhibited my natural motherly concerns. Thankfully, we knew they were in good hands. There is no way to repay friends who sacrifice as they did. It seems to be all the more meaningful when you're in such a desperate situation.

These back spasms were like being in labor with no epidural: intractable, severe, uncontrollable, and very weakening. Whether from drugs or weakness, I remember it taking all my effort to get liquid up the straw and into my mouth. I wished they would've put me in a medically induced coma until they figured out what to do with me. I guess they thought I'd get better; I only got weaker and weaker.

Once my doctor stopped by my room on his way to a surgery to help someone else. Uncharacteristically, I gathered strength from somewhere and lashed out at him for doing nothing to help me.

I was given all kinds of pain medication during those days. If they took the edge off, I didn't notice. However, these various drugs gave me various reactions: a strong, very rapid heartbeat, a sense of pulling of my head in different directions, spinning, and a sense that the building was moving, etc. Some of these side-effects, drug interactions, and pain made me feel like I was dying. After all that I went through during this hospital stay, I dreaded ever going back to a hospital during subsequent flare-ups. No variety or dosage of drugs seemed to help, but that catheter was a huge blessing!

Eventually, Dr. Uzcategui bought into the idea that the sacroiliac joint was the pain-generator. After a week of wasting away, he decided to fuse my right SI joint. I don't think that he was terribly convinced that this was the right thing to do, but he saw no other options. (Back in those days, this kind of surgery would require me to be put in a body cast for six weeks). Hoping for more insight, my doctor decided to do an electromyogram (EMG) to learn what he could about the health of my nerves and muscles.

Tim was not at all in favor of them fusing this SI joint. The muscle contractions that I had were so strong that in past flare-ups, we could see my vertebrae pulled out of alignment. We knew that the contractions I was having now would compromise the fusion. At that time, there was no talk of using screws to hold things in place while the bone graft took place over the course of several weeks. I couldn't reason through any of this. I was desperate; I just wanted something to be done!

I cannot imagine what this time must have been like for my dear husband, helpless to help me. He sat, stood, and paced by my side day after day. He remembered one day when I suddenly flattened out in a "stiff-as-a-board" and "eyes rolling back" type of seizure. Why this abnormal change in the brain's electrical activity? Was it possibly the result of the pain and the drugs? What a scary time this must have been for him, though he voiced none of that. In the solitude of the bathroom in my hospital room, he confessed to at least one meltdown session with Jesus. What would pull me out of this vortex? He begged Jesus for help. We both believed Jesus could heal me in a flash!

Because of my impending surgery to fuse this joint, they had given me an enema earlier in the day. When a nurse came into my room and announced that they would soon be taking me somewhere for this EMG, she must have seen fear wash over me. (Keep in mind, all communication with the nurses was in Spanish. I wasn't able to think, process, and speak much at all in English, let alone Spanish, especially with new medical terms being spoken.) Surprisingly, a nurse came back with the biggest diaper I'd ever seen and began to put it on me. Lord, have mercy! She thought my fear was what may happen while I was out having my test. Oh no! No! No! My objection to taking this test was the assault of being moved onto a gurney and all the bumps and turns to get to the test. If I couldn't tolerate anyone touching me or bumping my bed, how could I possibly handle a trip on a gurney? Nevertheless, they won; it was horrendous!

On a Wednesday, two weeks after arriving in the ER, a neurosurgeon who had studied pain management in China came into my hospital room. After meeting me, he began electro-acupuncture. This treatment operates on principles similar to manual acupuncture. The doctor inserted very thin needles all down my back and a few into my legs. Leads from the needles were connected to a device that allowed electrical current into my body for a 30-minute treatment.

This treatment was the first form of relief I'd had in two weeks! There was no doubt in my mind; God had sent this man our way. I had my second treatment the next day. After the third treatment, we asked that all medications be stopped. The next three days, my husband began manipulating the sacroiliac joint in place, as I could now tolerate touch! I needed frequent adjusting. After receiving five electric acupuncture treatments, I was able to begin eating, urinating, and walking. We received the help from God that we had been begging Him for. I was then discharged.

With the colossus of pain gone, I was left with a burning sensation running up and down my spine; it felt as though someone was continually rubbing a sunburn. Weird. This hospital experience left me with all the ingredients necessary for the making of post-traumatic stress disorder.

After several days of rest, we bravely made our way to the airport to fly back to the United States to recover and seek out more help. I was wheeled everywhere and allowed to lie down on the floor of the plane for the five-hour flight to the JFK airport in New York. I'd always been fearful of heights and flying, but I never let my children know. Now my fear of free-falling in a crash paled in the face of a long-drawn-out death from pain. How my perspectives on many things began to change in light of what I had just experienced and what was to come!

No doubt, we could have been arrested for all the syringes, needles, and narcotics we had with us. But after what I had just been through, I was not about to travel without that kind of help. I looked so wan and weak that I didn't think being arrested would a problem.

The airport attendant zoomed my wheelchair through non-public elevators and empty corridors as if they were in a hurry to get me out of there.

Just like that, our years in Venezuela were over with no goodbyes, no memorabilia, no journals, no possessions. Only the clothes that Jessica had packed. But I had what mattered: my precious family — and they still had me.

A Closer Look at the POWERFUL and ALL LOVING

Being far more powerful than the things He has made; my omnipotent Creator is never helpless to intercept and deliver me. All means are at His disposal to step in at any point to rescue me. God's arm is never too weak to liberate me; that comforts me, though it can be extremely hard to understand why He may choose not to. Some things are not for me to know, at least not yet. While God has stepped into time and has rescued His people on numerous occasions, that is the exception, not the norm. I need to remember that He's not obligated to do so.

As for being loving, God wouldn't have come in human form and spread His arms on a cursed Roman cross if He didn't love me! God determines my needs in my afflictions and supplies for them.

Charles Spurgeon said, "I have learned to kiss the wave that throws me up against the Rock of Ages." Could it be God's love that allows the circumstances that require me to live in dependence on Him?

"Seeing that He is clothed with omnipotence, no prayer is too hard for Him to answer, no need too great for Him to supply, no passion too strong for Him to subdue; no temptation too powerful for Him to deliver from, no misery too deep for Him to relieve."[6] A.W. Pink

CHAPTER 3

Desperate Times, Desperate Measures
APRIL 1996-FEBRUARY 1997

We arrived in Pennsylvania and settled in with my stepmom in my childhood home. Since I could no longer educate our children, much less make them breakfast, we had them jump into the last quarter of the school year at our church's private school. Because the school had a half-day kindergarten, they allowed us to put Julie in the first-grade class so that she could be there all day. This was not an optimal choice, but none of this was about having things our way; it was about surviving this crisis to the best of our ability.

I wasted no time setting up appointments. The first stop was an appointment with my chiropractor, Dwight, and my second was an orthopedic doctor at a large medical center an hour away. After I gave that doctor a snapshot of the last couple of years, he simply said, "You need a physical therapist specializing in the sacroiliac joint. I'm sorry, but I don't know of any." So, I took my script to a local physical therapist who recommended another physical therapist, Vince, who was an hour away. I didn't care how far I needed to travel or how hard I needed to work at rehabilitation. I'd be all in if someone could just show me the pathway to pain-free living.

My first of many years' appointments with Vince was very encouraging. We drove home with his words, "I can help you," ringing in our ears. And indeed, he did help! However, before Vince could begin working on my back, he had to address the iliopsoas (hip flexor) muscles in the front of my pelvis. These muscles connect the lower and upper body, allowing us to stand, walk, and move in all different angles. My psoas muscles were rock hard. He said it was evident that I'd been this way for a very long time. My pelvis was so dysfunctional that he had to show me how to move it. Because that movement meant pain, I had subconsciously shut it off years ago. I spent the next several weeks massaging those psoas muscles. Once they were supple, I could begin the stretching stage and then move on to the strengthening phase.

The main functions of those psoas muscles are to stabilize the spine, flex the hip (lift the leg), and stabilize the spine (preventing the vertebrae from rotating in the frontal plane). For the spine and hips to move naturally, without pain, the psoas has to be able to lengthen. And here is the culprit: the majority of our modern population has chronically tight (short) psoas muscles because we sit for 10-12 hours, day in and day out. Shortened muscles hinder optimal structural alignment. Some people go from sitting in class or the office all day, straight into high-intensity workouts with misaligned structures. Many activities, like cycling, spinning, Stairmaster, treadmill, and weight machines, add insult to injury by actually shortening the psoas muscle. No wonder many of us have problems with our lower back, pelvis, and hips.

As a child, I loved to swim, and as a teen, I regularly went to the YMCA to swim laps and play racquetball. I knew it would be a good idea to reinstate my membership. That first day back at the YMCA was memorable. I walked from one end of the pool to the other with no pain! It was my first physical movement without pain in a very long time! The buoyancy and resistance of the water made it the safest place for me to work my muscles. I often wished there was some way I could live the rest of my life in water if I couldn't get this issue resolved. Stretching and swimming felt so good! But I learned a lesson the hard way: I could still overdo it and hurt myself in the water if I wasn't careful.

Stretching and exercising outside the water was a three-hour-a-day commitment because I needed a lot of rest between the repetitions. But it was a welcome change to be able to take proactive steps toward healing. I was determined to do everything as prescribed so that I could get better as soon as possible. I desperately wanted to get back into life; we had three kids to raise!

Tim no longer needed to pound on my right SI joint to reposition the ilium up-slip. He only had to push on it, which was a lot better for those embarrassing adjustments that had to be done around other people. Tim couldn't help with my rotated sacrum, so we went to the chiropractor once or twice a week for that problem and for the issues in my neck. When Dwight hooked me up to his Transcutaneous Electrical Nerve Stimulation (TENS) device, the pain immediately lessened. Since the TENS unit was so helpful, I ordered my own. Though it was way better than Tylenol, it was certainly no cure.

A TENS unit is a battery-operated device, about the size of a deck of cards, that produces small electrical impulses through electrodes that have adhesive pads that you put on the skin over your pain area. These electrical impulses flood the nervous system, reducing its ability to transmit pain signals to the spinal cord and brain. These impulses also encourage the production of natural pain relievers called endorphins.

Vince gave me a sacroiliac belt to be worn around my hips to help stabilize my sacroiliac joints. Unlike the broad elastic back braces that support muscles, this belt stabilized my pelvic bones. The SI belt was a game-changer; I was finally able to move forward with exercise. He gave me a second belt to wear when swimming in the pool.

Wearing that belt 24/7 was a two-edged sword. To be profitable, I had to wear it tight, but that made it irritating. I would subconsciously take it off in my sleep, waking up in pain from no longer being aligned. Though I had a love/hate relationship with that thing, I wished I had owned one years ago!

At every appointment, Vince asked how I was doing. It was hard to know how to answer; the change was subtle. After several weeks I remember telling him things such as: "I ate dinner at the table with my family. I went up the stairs without thinking about it. I feel ten years younger than when I first came here." But I still didn't feel like I was in my thirties; people in their thirties don't need to sit down on the toilet to brush their teeth.

After several months of physical therapy, I had two good weeks! Those weeks brought us a glimmer of hope of returning to

Venezuela, but that glimmer certainly didn't qualify me for the trip to the airport.

For the same reason that one would eventually need to wean off crutches, Vince suggested that I stop wearing the SI belt. It seemed like good counsel. Besides, whatever he did for me was working! Unfortunately, we soon discovered that this situation was by no means under control. Subtly, I got worse. I can't remember if it was just days or weeks until I was in a massive flare-up with horrendous pain. I needed to go to the emergency room.

Having gone through all that I did in the hospital in Caracas when I couldn't get my pain under control for weeks on end, I knew it was critical to get on top of it; but I couldn't. I hated the thought of going to the hospital. They would put me through rounds of meaningless testing, which would show no culprit for the pain. And what would their choice of treatment do to me?

My other issue with going to the hospital was getting there. If someone barely bumping my mattress was so offensive, being in a moving car with turns and bumps was frightening! I'd been there and done that six months ago. Besides, there was nothing in the hospital that helped me with this level of pain before, only the electric acupuncture.

Just before we left for the emergency room, I remembered my SI belt! God must have put that thought in my fuzzy brain! *Why hadn't we thought of that earlier?* As soon as I secured that belt around my pelvis, my pain level began to drop! I was able to avoid going to the hospital, which was a sweet victory for me! This incident spoke volumes to us about the root of my pain, but it didn't seem significant to any of the professionals we told.

Our family physician had referred me to both orthopedic and pain management doctors. The pain management doctor was rough and gruff with me. After examining me, he said that I was depressed. His advice: "Get up each morning, make your bed, and stay out of it!" Ouch! I sure wished I could!

My experience with the orthopedic doctor was equally humiliating. The whole idea of the SI joint being hypermobile was preposterous to him. At the time, orthopedics generally didn't embrace the SI joint as being a significant contributor to low back pain. I'd heard over and over from orthopedists that the SI joint "doesn't move" or that "its movement is so slight that it couldn't be the cause." I now have a bundle of reports, including ones from the Second Interdisciplinary World Congress on Low Back Pain and the North American Spine Society, that says the opposite. (I spoke with this orthopedic doctor's partner years later, and he admitted that they had been in the dark concerning the dysfunction of the SI joint.)

Early in the 20th century, any pain in the lower back, buttock, and leg was diagnosed as sacroiliac joint syndrome. It was called the "Era of the SI Joint" because so many doctors believed that the SI joint was the cause of most back problems. However, in 1932, with the discovery of the herniation and ruptured disk, the "Dynasty of the Disk" was born. This caused the death of the SI joint diagnosis. In the 1980s, some physicians rediscovered the SI joint as the possible source of back pain and has been referred to as the "underappreciated" cause of lower back, pelvic, and lower extremity pain.

We told the orthopedic doctor about the prescription narcotics that we had brought back to America. I had been taking them for the last couple of weeks. Of course, the doctor saw nothing that would warrant all the pain medication I was taking. I'm sure alarms of abuse were going off in his mind. I had gone through several more prescriptions for narcotics, muscle relaxants, and anti-inflammatory drugs from my primary care physician. Growing up, a little bottle of aspirin must have lasted our family of six a decade; we just weren't pill-poppers. I was conservative with medication, knowing that narcotics could become a slippery slope for anyone. Therefore, Tim kept a record of all the pills I took. I wanted to be vigilant and set a good example for our kids. I also wanted to have a healthy liver down the road. My orthopedic doctor told me that he currently had a patient with a crushed pelvis and that I was "supposedly" in more pain than she was. Therefore, my situation made no sense to him, apart from my being crazy.

Over the next couple of weeks, when the orthopedic doctor saw that I was not getting any better, he told me that there was "no reason for your pain" and that I was "doing all this for attention." If this was a matter of getting attention, I could have dreamed up something much less expensive! He recommended that I go to a psychiatric hospital for treatment. Though I was just too weak, in every way, to respond to his assessment, his words lingered in my mind for years. I allowed his words to hurt me until I finally chose to forgive him for his ignorance. And that's all it was, a lack of understanding. I'm sure he wanted to help me but just didn't have the know-how.

It was growing apparent to me that there wasn't anyone who could put an end to this. In addition to wearing the SI belt, I now wore two TENS units because of significant muscle spasms in my neck.

Physical therapy and chiropractic treatments were temporary treatments with effects that often wore off on the ride back home. Having tried all the mainstream medical options that we were aware of, we turned to various alternative medicine routes. Ideally, we wanted to find an acupuncturist who could do electric acupuncture, since it was so successful back in Caracas. This being the pre-internet era, we couldn't locate anyone who did this.

Desperate for relief, Tim and I found the acupuncture needles the doctor in Caracas had left with us and decided to use them with my TENS units. Avoiding the spine, Tim inserted the thin, flexible needles in random places in my back, and placed the sticky conductive TENS pads over top of them. We had success with our homemade electroacupuncture kit, though it was not as beneficial as the treatments that the doctor in Caracas gave me. Desperate times call for desperate measures.

In the early years, Tim was always giving me back rubs. Then there were years that I didn't want him to rub my back. But during those years, Tim began grabbing the skin in the area of my spasm and pulling it upward. The muscle obviously is attached to the skin, and this way of stretching the muscle would give me a short relief from the spasm. The problem was he couldn't keep a grip on my skin. I kept thinking that a clamp would work. We were crazy enough to try it, but it didn't work. Then Tim came up with the great idea of using pine tar. Pine tar sticks are marketed for baseball players because it helps them get a good grip on the bat. Tim would warm up the end of the stick and rub some of it on his hands. The tar gave him a good enough grip to pull on those muscles effectively.

Sometimes, at the onset of a flare-up, I felt the need for my muscles to be pulled, but wouldn't want to ask Tim. I usually tried to hide my pain from him, hoping that I would feel better before he knew I hurt. Lying down in bed didn't always mean I was in a flare-up, especially if I was reading a book and could smile when he walked into the room. It was a stupid game. He reads me so well; he knows when I'm in pain by looking into my eyes and by observing my movements. I always wanted Tim to think I was better than I was so he wouldn't worry about me.

To be honest, there was another reason why I didn't want Tim to know when I was in pain. I didn't want to get a little "talking-to." Truly, he always had my best interest at heart. But I guarantee you, I already went over all the "I should have" and the "I shouldn't have" lines on my own. What we usually overlooked were the hundreds of right choices I had made compared to the devastating wrong decisions I had made. For me, pain breeds guilt. Even though I know it shouldn't, it does. Deep down, I felt like I should've been able to manage this beast.

Trials of great magnitude usually bring couples closer together or push them apart. Thankfully these trials drove Tim and I closer to one another and to God. I had a terribly dark season of depression when I felt abandoned by God. I believe my dear husband was the conduit of God's grace: protecting, providing, comforting, and loving me!

Friends of ours hired Tim for appliance deliveries. Thankfully, they were very gracious to allow him flexibility with his hours, as I needed him to take me to appointments since I couldn't sit up to drive myself. Sometimes I needed him home because I was having such a hard time managing my pain and emotions. Many times, the comfort of my husband's presence and words of truth helped deflect a panic attack. He faithfully walked closely by my side through this entire mess. What a priceless gift!

Tim is an excellent maintenance man, but he couldn't fix any of this. During the first year of this saga, the back pain was entirely my problem. But after that year, Tim began to learn how to shoulder this burden with me. Ever since then, he's been deeply committed to me in every way. I have such a gem of a husband; he is the flip to my flop!

When I contemplate the many ways that he has served me through the years, the gift of attentive listening is probably the most treasured. I had a genuine need to stop stuffing my feelings and start identifying and externalizing my pent-up emotions. Saturated with all different kinds of hurt, chronic pain sufferers need a trusted friend or two to come along beside them to help mop up the pain that puddles around them by listening. A friend may feel completely clueless as to how to help but listening with a caring heart is invaluable. Understand that absorbing a portion of the pain is some of the best medicine out there. There were a few times in this tumultuous year when I feared that my incessant dejection would push Tim over the edge and that I would lose my lifeline. However, all that fear was in vain; like a huge boulder, he wasn't about to budge. I couldn't imagine a better man for me.

I didn't know how to turn off the overwhelming panic and angst that threatened to undo me. Denying my feelings never helped, and shifting my focus was like trying to stop an 18-wheeler on a decline. I was not strong enough to do so on my own.

Though Tim could easily detect the lies I was falling for and point me back to truth, just rattling off instructions about what I should be thinking didn't help. Over time, we discovered together the importance of both venting and validating my feelings before speaking the truth in love.

For example, I would tell Tim: "I feel like such a lousy wife and mother, not able to do anything with or for the kids. They leave the house with unbrushed hair and mismatched socks. I'm so afraid I won't sleep again tonight. This whole situation frustrates me beyond words. When will this come to an end? Will it? Though He said He would never leave me, I feel abandoned by God."

Tim would listen to me vent and cry; he learned to validate my feelings. But then, after about ten minutes or so of that, he would direct my thinking toward the truth. He knew that dwelling on those negative feelings would drive me further south, so he lovingly guided our conversation toward the objective truth.

He would say: "You're not a lousy wife and mother, Kerri. You are sick. You obviously can't do the things for us that you want to do. But you are loving us the best you can right now. Though it feels like God has forsaken you, He hasn't."

Then I would grab onto the truth that he had expounded on, at least for a little while. My mind was the battlefield, and I was fighting for truth. In the thick of things, when I was losing mental stability, we probably had a session or two every day. My impaired thoughts seemed imprisoned to my lying emotions. Being spoon-fed bite-sized pieces of truth helped set me free. Thankfully, my husband became adept at this process.

The longer I traveled this road, the less hope I had of healing. I was still in a huge mess: bedridden, a constant high level of back pain, little to no sleep (and nightmares when I did), no appetite, no help from the medical community, and memories from that hospital experience six months ago. And now, tears! Oh, how the tears flowed! At first, it seemed as if I was making up for all the years that I had stuffed my feelings. Because this ordeal had stolen so much from me physically, I had fought hard to keep it from invading my emotions, but that was a losing battle.

One question I have grown to hate over the years is "What's your pain level right now?" Answering that would depend on what the asker understood those numbers to indicate. So, I developed my own scale:

> Level 1: I'm aware.
> Level 2: I need to lie down now, or things will get much worse.
> Level 3: Get on ice!
> Level 4: Time for the TENS unit.
> Level 5: I need narcotics.
> Level 6: I don't know what I need. Don't ask me any questions!
> Level 7: I'm having flashbacks of horrible bouts of pain.
>   I need distraction!
> Level 8: Lamaze breathing technique — unless I'm too weak.
> Level 9: Don't touch my bed and definitely don't touch me!
> Level 10: I think I'm dying, or I want to be dead.

The pain management doctor was right about one thing; I was depressed. People from all walks of life and personalities can succumb to depression. Our bodies don't endure high levels of pain and stress unscathed. Emotional and mental fallout was inevitable.

Apart from wrong thinking on my part, I believe that my body had been in survival mode for so long that it was running out of the resources it needed to maintain itself. As hard as I fought, I couldn't will the tears away; I was powerless to stop them. A deluge of sadness overwhelmed me through the long hours I cried each day for weeks on end. I didn't know where all these painful feelings were coming from, but I needed them to stop tormenting me.

Months later, I realized that I was grieving the loss of many things. I couldn't process the death of my dear dad when he died the year before. We had no closure to the loss of our lives in Venezuela. There was vexation from knocking on so many doors of the medical world with no resolution and from being misunderstood time and again. Then a friend finally turned on the spotlight: "Kerri, you're grieving the loss of your health!"

I had so much physical and emotional pain, that it seemed like one big cyclone. I found it helpful to identify the difference sources of my pain and learn the difference between grief and self-pity.

Feelings of grief originate from loss. When we allow ourselves to experience those feelings, we move along in the process of mourning, which helps us accept the loss. But self-pity, which is very common in grief, keeps us focused on the negative and is oblivious to any good. Unlike grief, we wallow in self-pity by choice and refuse to learn anything positive from our pain.

It seemed like my mind and body moved in slow motion, with a fragile connection between the two. I struggled to do the simplest of things, like eating and brushing my teeth. Life was being filtered through my dark emotions; my objectivity was gone with the wind. I could not make decisions or reason. Truth was a vanishing illusion. It was scary being so out of control of my thinking. I just bounced between thick fog and darkness, with no bright side to look on. This whole new realm of suffering, coupled with the physical torment, was pulling me under quickly. Up until this point, I had no idea that emotional pain could be as equally severe as physical pain.

There was yet another crucial sphere of my life that this trial now invaded: my spiritual being. I was utterly unprepared for the all-encompassing profound suffering I was up against. At my very weakest, the Enemy of my soul implanted his murderous lies in my mind: *"You've suffered terribly. God's been silent. Why would a God Who claims to devoutly love you allow such profound suffering and for so long? He has all the power to stop it, but He doesn't. He must not truly love you. Take control and end this yourself."*

The Deceiver was making a substantial argument for his case. Then, in a very weakened condition from ongoing uncontrollable pain, very little food, and absolutely no sleep for a couple of days, a mental image flashed into my mind with the concept of just how to end this anguish.

When my suffering was more than I could bear and when God didn't deliver me as I thought He should have, the bedrock of my trust in God succumbed to a seismic quake. I had a lot of heavy questions for God: *Apart from suicide, where is my escape? Where is the peace that You promised me? How could You possibly use this for my good when all of this has ruined me? Why is there no inkling of Your presence? Why are You hiding from me? Is this what **love** looks like?*

My disappointment with God turned to disillusionment, which was an insecure and scary place for me. And the longer my physical, emotional, mental, and spiritual pain lingered, the more the answers mattered. I felt ashamed of myself for wrestling with God over these things. But Tim wasn't surprised or bothered by it. He said he would be worried if I weren't struggling. As long as I was struggling with these issues, he knew that I cared about spiritual things.

I knew God welcomed me to come to Him to lament. I knew He understood my anger, frustration, and rage. But I didn't want to go to Him, because I was losing my desire to trust Him. I still believed that He loved everyone else in the world, but now I doubted that He loved *me*. Though that seems ridiculous to me now, that is what my darkened mind was thinking. Though I knew better than to base my theology on feelings, as feelings change with the tide, it was a battle to not let my feelings take over. Although my understanding of God's love for me was rooted in objective truth — on what He had done for me, not on my impressions — the battle raged within me.

Though I doubted God's love, I never doubted His ability to heal me. I just couldn't understand why He wasn't rescuing me. I was ashamed of the suicidal thoughts I was having. I didn't want to tell Tim that I had a plan to take my life, but I knew I needed help. Although I thought Tim could understand my desire to take my own life, I knew our children would never understand. It would undermine everything I'd ever taught them about trusting God, shattering them to their cores and possibly creating severe consequences for the rest of their lives. Love takes on different forms at different times in our lives. In this time of sore temptation, loving my kids meant holding on for just the next hour. Though I wouldn't hesitate to die for my kids, choosing to live hour by hour in those days seemed way more sacrificial.

January 1997

Oh God,

Praying doesn't seem to be changing things, but these things are changing me. So, help me! I give You this whole mess. I doubt You when what You have allowed is so hard! This pain scares me. I'm so weak in every way. You say You won't give me more than I can bear without Your help, but it seems to me like You have, yet I know You are not a liar. Holding on is probably the best gift I can give

Jessica, Jonathan, Julie, and Tim. They need the example of trusting You in the middle of the bitterness of life. Perhaps the most important thing I can do for them is to keep on believing You. So, help me not give up! I want to trust You, but this pain is terrifying; I need courage. I need Your mercy because I am undone.

Kerri

With my mental capacities wrecked, my emotions in torment, my body in agony, and my spirit hopeless, I lost my ability to hold on. Honestly, I was surprised that not even my fierce love for my precious family was enough to enable me to hold on. When that last thread of hope slipped through my fingers, I discovered that Someone was holding on to me!

Apart from the pain, I had everything I could ever want, all those wonderfully satisfying things that money can't buy: a wonderful marriage, awesome kids, a loving and faithful family, and friends.

I wanted to live my life for the purposes for which my Creator had made me. And I was finding joy in that journey! But brutal pain now infected every aspect of my life. Though I had fought valiantly from every angle, it seemed I was mortally wounded. Any determination to persevere, any strength to hold out, and any ways to conquer evil were not within me. I had reached the very end of me. I was not strong enough to hold on through the fierce storm. In fact, I had no strength apart from what God gave me. But when did I ever? I've never been able to provide my next breath.

Tim said, "Well, Kerri, you can't get any lower." I don't know if he said that for my benefit or his. Getting worse had become a growing fear of mine. Over the years, every single time I thought that I was at the bottom of the pit, I discovered that the pit was still deeper. So, his statement comforted me. That day, I told Tim not to leave me alone. Then he asked me if I was done trying to cope. I answered him truthfully. Immediately he was on the phone with our doctor. There was no waiting for this appointment. I was ushered straight to the doctor and asked some hard questions. She told me that the antidepressant medication would take about six weeks to be fully working in my system. To that, I remember thinking, *"I can't possibly last days, let alone weeks."* Although it took months to find the right combination and dosage of antidepressants that worked best for me, in the first three days of taking an antidepressant, I was finally able to sleep instead of catnapping, and I could swallow food much easier. I could begin to fight again.

I was a good girl. Yet I knew I was a profound sinner; I didn't need to be convinced of that. But I never thought I was capable of committing murder. Being suicidal gave me a front-row seat to my capabilities. Having survived those days of temptation by absolutely no merit of my own, I have a better understanding of myself. We are all individual cookies made from the same lump of sinful dough. Now when I see someone's sin spewed across the newspaper, I can identify with them, because I now know, experientially, that my flesh is capable of any sin, even murder. Knowing this knocked me right off a pedestal that I didn't realize I was on! Every humbling experience, painful as it is, is so good for me. It keeps convincing me of how utterly broken and desperately needy I truly am.

February 1997

Dear God,

There's a wall between us. What do I do with my disillusionment? My bitterness? My unbelief? Confess it and move on? How do I do that? You cannot be unfaithful, but because I perceive that You've been, I'm holding a grudge. After all, You have allowed such devastation! I felt scrapped — like a writer's crumbled up ideas discarded into the circular file. Did I believe You were out of control just because I was? Help me tear down this wall of resentment — brick by brick. I don't know what the bricks are or how to dislodge them. Help me! I don't have the wisdom to fix this, so I'm asking for some of Yours.

I've never been so empty in all my life. But empty doesn't mean abandoned. Numb doesn't mean I'll never feel again. Fallen doesn't mean I've quit. Crushed doesn't mean I'm discarded. I can't wait for positive feelings to come; I could be waiting a lifetime. I can't live a meaningful, contented life without You, my best Friend. I hate this emptiness, discouragement, and apathy! I don't have to feel to believe; I'm learning that. Help me learn to trust You even when I'm enshrouded in utter darkness. I can't sense Your love, peace, or presence, but my perception doesn't change the realities any more than the clouds remove the sun.

You will never fit into the mold that I make for You, and that's a very good thing. How could the finite possibly figure out the infinite? I don't want this wall between us. Why couldn't I realize You wanted me? Was it because I thought with my feelings? Renew my thinking and align it with Your truth.

- *Regardless of how I perceive You, You are good through and through.*
- *Regardless of whether what You do seems right to me, You are completely righteous.*
- *Regardless of what You permit, You are just.*
- *Regardless of whether You seem loving to me today, You are love.*
- *Regardless of what I choose to believe about You, You cannot make a mistake, not even one. You are perfection.*

Remove my doubt. Calm my fears. Revive my love. I want to want You back in my life!

Kerri

Thankfully, weeks down the road, the antidepressant medication was at work, helping me feel a lot better. I knew recovery was going to take quite some time; I had time. The deeper the wound, the longer the healing. Seeing progress, no matter how slow, was very rewarding. Weight-bearing activity, my own weight that is, continued to cause pain, but I eventually reached the point where I could lie on the floor or in a recliner without pain. What *sweet* relief!

Now that I was physically doing better, I could begin the process of emotional and spiritual healing as well. But I wasn't the only one in the family dealing with the fallout. Jessica was deeply hurting from the cataclysmic events that rocked her world in 1996. Being older, she remembers more of those days than Jonathan and Julie. She has some good advice for parents who are raising children amid crises.

Dear Parent,

This letter is for you who suffer from chronic pain along with the responsibility of raising children. Let me start by saying, I am so sorry. It's not fair. This is not how it was supposed to be.

Our Heavenly Father sees and weeps alongside you. Your children experience this injustice along with you. You are going through pain which causes your children pain. Yet because you're suffering with in-your-face pain, you may not be able to see your child's pain.

I can only imagine the grief of a parent in chronic pain, unable to be the parent they want to be. But I do, however, know firsthand the pain of a child whose parent is, practically speaking, an absent parent due to their physical pain. I could stuff and ignore my pain, my mom could not. I could function and move in my pain, but my mom could not.

I lived in the shadow of a mountain, hidden and hurting. I felt my pain was trivial, and I didn't feel free to express it. But it wasn't insignificant, it was very real. My anger and confusion grew. My mother was often bedridden in incredible pain, followed by either a medicated fog or emotional instability. Being a good husband, my father gave his attention to my needy mom. I fell to the wayside. I lost out on what could have been, with both of them. By the grace of God, I survived.

But what can you do to help your child when you are in the midst of chronic suffering? First, acknowledge your child's pain. Give it validity; it is as real as yours. I knew my mother's physical pain was not my fault; but I felt that my pain was my fault. I felt as if I had no right to hurt because no one had done anything wrong. But if your child feels as if they've been ignored or neglected, it is vital to admit that you have let them down or failed them. When you take the blame for their pain, you are giving your child a sense of freedom to express their pain without its being trivialized. You are giving them a platform to leap off into healing.

Second: Help your child develop meaningful relationships with other adults that are safe to talk with and that can help shoulder their disappointment, grief, and pain. Set aside any jealousy and independence. Assure your child that they are not betraying you but that you want them to talk freely with godly adults who can help them process their pain. What a gift you are giving them!

Sincerely,

Jessica

It was very hard to learn of my daughter's deep and hidden pain decades later, realizing that there was yet more that this tragedy stole. I'm grateful that my daughter shared these insights and am hopeful that they may help others.

With most physical injuries, one can usually anticipate the amount of time needed to heal and can prepare for it. But there's no predicting the length of time necessary for emotional and mental recovery. I asked God for complete healing and didn't care how long it would take. I just wanted it to be thorough, as it would be better to deal with festering pockets of resentment and bitterness now rather than have them erupt further down life's road. So, for the next couple of years, I worked to reconcile my feelings with the truth. *(See Appendix for Feelings versus Truth.)*

A Closer Look at the EVER PRESENT

When I was most aware of my need for God, I couldn't sense His presence. I imagined that He was playing some kind of sick game of hide-and-seek. In my deep depression, the only thing I could feel was pain and profound sadness.

While I always want to sense God's love and care for me, feelings were never meant to hold me up. While it may be hard to grasp in the middle of a storm, objective truth from the Bible does not lie. It says: God is present everywhere (Psalm 139:7-10), darkness is as light to Him (Psalm 139:12), everything is uncovered and laid bare before Him (Hebrews 4:13), and the highest heaven cannot contain Him (I Kings 8:27). God is closer than my pain, closer than I can imagine. He said that He is a very present help in trouble (Psalm 34:18) and will never leave nor forsake me (Hebrews 13:5). So, when my senses fail to perceive His presence with me, I have to rest in the promise of Psalm 34:18, "The Lord is close to the brokenhearted and saves those who are crushed in spirit."

CHAPTER 4

You Can't Live Like This!
1999-2004

Family and friends could not understand why the medical community could not help me. And frankly, neither could I. The only abnormality my workup revealed was a bulging disc between L4 and L5. Big deal. Who doesn't have at least one?

Why not just fuse the SI joint? I lived with chronic pain, the kind you can't "push through," which confined me to bed for weeks and months. For the life of me, I couldn't imagine that kind of debilitation being a better option than fusion. Besides, the SI joint hardly has any movement. Either my medical professionals did not understand how debilitating this was, or they didn't know how to help me. I wondered all the time, *if this nation could put a man on the moon, why can't the medical community do something to stabilize my joint?*

As I grew more acquainted with this problem, I discovered that an issue with the sacroiliac wasn't such a rare ailment, but the degree to which I suffered truly was.

The next couple of years were problematic. With the hard iliopsoas muscles now softened, I'd lost my inner crutch. Attempting to replace that "hardened" soft tissue with toned and strengthened muscles without triggering spasms was extremely frustrating. Wearing the SI belt around the clock helped with my stability, and the swimming helped strengthen my muscles so I could be a little more active. But my muscles needed to be strong enough to support movement outside of the water where life happened. I continued to bounce from one flare-up to the next. Each flare-up was a vortex of all-encompassing back and neck spasms, bloating, bowel cramping, and headaches. Over the years I developed an instruction sheet to help me deal with my flare-ups. *(See Appendix.)*

Every month, the hormone relaxin (which relaxes pelvic ligaments when it's time for a woman to give birth) had a loosening effect during my menstrual cycle. But it was ten years later that I learned that the release of this hormone made me more prone to injury.

Although my health care professionals did their best to help me, it seemed like we were just putting adhesive bandages on a gaping wound.

In April of 1999, Vince, my physical therapist, recommended that we visit one of his former teachers at the Spine Clinic at the Pittsburg University Medical Center. There, I had two simple tests that I had never had before: standing X-rays in various positions, and a homemade level. The level rested on my hips, revealing either the balance or imbalance of my pelvic bones. On my initial appointment, the pelvis looked balanced. However, when the level test was repeated the next day, the doctor was shocked! "What did you do?" he asked.

"Nothing," I replied. "I left your office, had the X-rays taken, and went straight back to the hotel. I was in bed for the rest of the day and this morning until this appointment."

He was flabbergasted.

"Wow!" he said. "I've seen this before, but not without major trauma! You can't live like this!"

Exactly! Someone with letters behind their name finally recognized my predicament! He gave me a C.A.S.H. (Cruciform Anterior Spinal Hyperextension) brace to wear. This three-point system restricts flexion and helps stabilize the spine. Unfortunately, this doctor said that he couldn't help me, but recommended that I visit both a prolotherapist and an orthopedic surgeon. According to him, prolotherapy and sacroiliac fusion were my only two options.

I'd already seen several orthopedic surgeons on this journey, so I wasn't keen on an appointment with yet another. But I made an appointment with the orthopedic doctor that he recommended. This orthopedist was also against the SI fusion. I'm sure if my sacrum or ilium were cracked or crushed, he'd do his utmost to repair it. They all would have.

Prolotherapy (short for "proliferative therapy") activates the body's natural healing mechanisms to build new tissue in damaged connective tissue, such as ligaments, tendons, and cartilage, which naturally have a low blood supply. Dozens of injections (of a proliferant agent — often just dextrose and Lidocaine) given all around the injury site bring about an inflammatory response. This tricks the body into another repair cycle, gradually building up new tissue to restore integrity to the injured joint.

Finding a proficient prolotherapist in those days was a trial in itself. But the third doctor we met with knew what he was doing. These prolotherapy treatments proved to be extremely helpful. The inflammation tightened the joint, enabling me to move without pain. These treatments allowed me to function normally as long as there was enough inflammation to tighten my joint. About five or six weeks after the last prolotherapy treatment, the muscle spasms and instability would return because the inflammation had gone down, and then I would need to go back for another round of treatment.

A year of prolotherapy treatments gave me a new lease on life. One day, Jonathan came home from school, took a look at me, and randomly said, "Hey, Mom, you don't look like a bed person!" I took that as a compliment. Attending baseball and soccer games were among my first outings. I loved watching my kids play! I could even sit up to ride in the car. I remember thinking, *Wow! I really like being with people!* I was even able to hold a part-time job at a nearby bank answering the phone. Finally, I could help with the family finances instead of being a drain.

The prolotherapist doctor was pleased with my progress, yet he was concerned about my neck. He didn't think my back problem would be resolved until my neck got help. I began seeing a different chiropractor who had a more comprehensive approach than my regular chiropractor. His masseuse told me that my back and neck were like cement. Well, if I were cement, she was a jackhammer!

During the fourth year of my prolotherapy treatments, the doctor began treating both of my SI joints, as now the left side was hyper-mobile as well.

My doctor said that he had never treated a patient as long as he had treated me. Since he was unsure of the long-term effects of so many treatments, he wanted me to wean me off these treatments. I had thought that it was taking my ligaments a long time to heal because they were so damaged. (Years later I read somewhere that if three to four treatments don't heal it, then prolotherapy never will.) I figured that weaning me off of the treatments would confine me to bed again.

And it did. I was back to living with debilitating pain. That sure put a damper on things. I had three teenagers to keep up with and feed! Tim and the kids were adjusting both SI joints several times a day. Though prolotherapy had worked wonders for me, it proved to only ever be a temporary fix.

One morning I forgot to put on my SI belt when I got out of bed. A couple of hours later, maddening pain began. I was bedridden for the next ten days. How discouraging!

The thought of fusing the joints came to the forefront of my mind. It seemed the only solution. But where in the world could we go to get these joints fused? How could we convince an orthopedic surgeon to fuse these joints? Orthopedic doctors need evidence that something is broken before they will fix it. All I had was a long relationship with pain, images that showed a healthy body, and my testimony of how prolotherapy, an unheard-of treatment, had helped.

Unlike the first decade of my problem, we now had access to the internet. When I was well enough to sit up at the computer with my SI belt on, I typed in "sacroiliac fusion." Gainesville Physical Therapy of Atlanta, Georgia, surfaced, with lots of pertinent information. I promptly sent them my medical history. I was utterly amazed to hear back via a personal phone call!

Specialist Vicki Sims, a compassionate physical therapist specializing in diagnosing and treating SIJD (sacroiliac joint dysfunction), was on the line. (Wow! My condition had a name, who knew?) When she assured me that there was indeed help for my issues, I quickly booked a flight to Atlanta.

The function of the sacroiliac joint is to provide stability for your body in weight-bearing positions: standing, sitting, and moving around. This complex pelvic "girdle" also plays a shock-absorbing role, distributing forces across the pelvis. Many different things can go wrong with this unique joint with its various axes of motion. It is called the "underappreciated" cause of low back pain for a good reason. Accurate diagnostic testing of this joint is difficult at best and has caused skepticism among many medical professionals. Many orthopedics believe that the SI joint cannot move enough to even cause a problem. Oh, the things that I can learn about SIJD now with a single touch of my finger that took us decades to learn.

For me, there was no single test that gave us a diagnosis of sacroiliac joint dysfunction. The Palpation and FABER tests did not immediately reproduce my pain. The classic lidocaine in the SI joint would have done nothing to aid in a diagnosis since my pain was in the lumbar region, not in the SI joint. I've read at Spine-Health.com that "Imaging tests such as X-rays, CT, and MRI are typically less helpful than clinical tests since pain responses cannot be imaged, and often, many abnormal imaging findings are non-symptomatic and/or not clinically relevant."[7] There is no single approach to diagnosing and managing SI joint pain that works for everyone, which can make getting help for this problem very difficult.

In Atlanta, I first met with Dr. Lippitt, the orthopedic surgeon that worked with Vicki Sims. As my litmus test for him, I decided that I would only tell him about the dysfunction in my right sacroiliac joint. I knew that I had issues with the left one as well, but I wondered if he would explore both joints or just give attention to my complaint. As I sat in an opened-back gown for the umpteenth time, I tried hard to guard my expectations. I was so hopeful, yet quite skeptical, and very nervous. After twelve long years of knocking on door after door, could this possibly be my last stop?

When Dr. Lippitt entered the room, he asked me a few questions before he began to move my legs around to see how my pelvis and hips functioned. Less than five minutes later, he told me to get dressed and left the room. Fear and hope collided within me, so that by the time Dr. Lippitt came back into the room to talk with me, I was struggling to hold back my tears. He immediately rambled off three things wrong with the right joint and two things wrong with the left. Then he simply stated, "We can help you. You need a double sacroiliac fusion."

There were no comments about my being crazy or doing this for attention; he assured me that I was at the mecca for this problem. No more tests ordered. He simply relied on his experienced hands to determine the function of those joints. Just like that, our twelve long years of searching were over. It was surreal! We had a diagnosis and a team who could fix the root of my dilemma. Can I say it? Finally!

"Subluxation," was the term Dr. Lippitt and Mrs. Sims used to describe what was happening to these joints. Joint dislocation is a "displacement of a bone from its natural position to the joint"; subluxation is "a partial dislocation." I was experiencing subluxation from hypermobility of the sacroiliac joint.

> "Subluxation occurs when a bone is partially pulled or pushed out of place (out of its normal relationship to the other bones that make up a joint). ... A subluxation may be caused by a direct blow to the joint, a fall, or a sudden twisting movement. Everyday activities may cause this injury if a person has unstable joints. ... [A] subluxation may [temporarily] feel better because the dislocated bone has partially popped back into place ... Soft tissues (such as ligaments, tendons, muscles, cartilage, and the joint capsule) in or around a joint may stretch or tear."[8]

Certainly, lax ligaments are easier to detect in more isolated joints. Sacroiliac joints are complex joints, working on various axes with many ligaments all over that significant weight-bearing region of the body. No doubt, my story seemed dubious because I had no injury per se; but I believe the hard blow from that seesaw way back in the '70s held some significance.

In 2004, Mrs. Sims published her book, *The Secret Cause of Low Back Pain*. This comprehensive self-help book explained what SIJD is and how you could effectively treat it. This book contained numerous illustrations and self-help tools that may prevent individuals with SIJD from moving to my level of dysfunction. If I'd had a resource like that book a decade prior, most likely I would've learned how to tame the beast before it got the best of me. Knowledge is power, and I was powerless against this malady.

Down through the years, when people would ask me how I felt, I came up with the phrase: "par for the course." It was honest enough, yet not negative. When people kindly asked what was wrong with me, I found it very frustrating to explain something that I struggled to understand. Eventually, this is how I explained my problem: If I placed a rubber band in front of you, you wouldn't know if it would be useful until you picked it up and used it to hold something together. Just by looking at the rubber band, you wouldn't necessarily be able to ascertain its ability to function. It seems to me that my ligaments were lot like that rubber band. The doctors looked at the joint and determined it was fine because nothing appeared to be wrong. However, when I used the joint, the ligaments weren't able to do their job. As a result, my muscles stepped up as a stand-in to offer support to the joint — but they weren't designed to do ligament work.

Most people with SIJD have pain directly in their SI joint; thus, every step they take gives them pain in the center of their buttock. These people often use crutches or wheelchairs to get around. The typical pre-surgery diagnostic testing for sacroiliac joint dysfunction is an injection of Lidocaine directly into the SI joint, the center of the buttock. The Lidocaine temporarily eliminates the pain, and the diagnosis is confirmed. But I didn't have pain in my buttocks. I had referred pain in my low back. With no pain in my buttock a shot of Lidocaine would have been useless. Thankfully Dr. Lippitt did not require that I have a positive diagnostic Lidocaine test before agreeing to operate.

But the battle wasn't over. Over the next twelve months, I was scheduled three times for the double SI fusion. The holdup every time was the insurance company. They continued to refuse coverage for this surgery, claiming that it was "experimental and investigational."

Dr. Lippitt was livid. Back then, most orthopedic doctors did not believe that subluxation could happen to this joint. But Dr. Lippitt knew differently; he printed out a passel of documentation for me to give to the insurance company to substantiate the need of this surgery.

Our insurance company required a second opinion. Since I had never met any other orthopedic surgeon willing to fuse these joints, I didn't have high expectations for that appointment. When I met with the only orthopedic surgeon at the Hersey Medical Center that preformed SI fusions, he flew through my documents and fired questions at me faster than I could answer. He concluded that fusing these joints would not help me. But he said that I had "done my homework." In other words, I had investigated and invested in every possible solution and had no more options.

He wasn't rude or insulting. Unlike the doctor who thought I was doing all this for attention, this doctor said that he believed my story stating: "You've got better things to do with your time." Dead on there!

When asked, I told him that I was planning on having this surgery regardless of his opinion. Though he made sure I knew he wasn't endorsing the surgery, saying that I met none of the criteria for this surgery, he went on to make the most honest, open-minded comment that I had ever heard from a doctor: "Who's to say that if I were in your shoes, I wouldn't be doing the same thing [having the surgery]."

Lacking a second opinion in support of the surgery, in January of 2004, Tim wrote the following letter to our health insurance company.

> *Dear Sirs,*
>
> *We received your letter regarding the First Level Grievance Committee Determination, dated November 24, 2003. Needless to say, we were disappointed to hear that this surgery was denied, again! You stated that this surgery would be "experimental/investigative." I looked up those words in the dictionary to make sure I understood your position.*
>
> *Experimental means: "Pertaining to experiment; founded on, or derived from experiment or trial."*
>
> *Investigational means: "The act or process of investigating; or a detailed inquiry or systematic examination."*
>
> *For the past 12 years, we have been heavily involved in precisely those two things. When Kerri's pain first started, we tried all the traditional treatments, muscle relaxants, bed rest, and pain killers. She has seen numerous orthopedic specialists and a plethora of other specialists. She has had all manner of testing, all of which showed nothing.*
>
> *This was when we entered the **experimental** phase. Finding little benefit from traditional medicine and desperate to end this pain, we started searching for alternative help. We tried magnets, iridology, raindrop therapy with essential oils, etc. That, sirs, was experimental.*
>
> *Now the **investigational** phase began. The first real help, apart from the narcotics — a temporary pacifier — was chiropractic treat-*

ments. Manipulations of the SI joint brought the first wave of relief — thousands of structural adjustments. We never saw more than a couple days of relief from thousands of structural alignments over many years. However, it did show us that the root of the problem lay somewhere in the sacroiliac joint.

Then we investigated physical therapy, which was helpful. Kerri faithfully worked to strengthen that whole area with the hopes of stabilizing that joint. Though beneficial, the results were quite limited. We were still very dependent on chiropractic adjustments to keep her pain level down.

While under the treatment of a physical therapist, we began to understand what was happening. Kerri's SI joint was hyper-mobile, causing it to lock in misalignment, stressing the lower back and causing muscle spasms. Properly adjusting and stabilizing it was the secret. Our next experiment was with a sacroiliac belt. Kerri needed to wear that belt so tight, it created its own set of problems. However, it did offer relief, showing us that stabilizing the SI joint was the key to solving this problem.

While still investigating and searching for something to bring an end to this pain, Dr. Richard Erhard at the spine clinic at the Pittsburg University Medical Center told us we had two options to treat this condition: an injection therapy known as prolotherapy or sacroiliac fusion.

No orthopedic was in favor of fusion in those days. So, we pursued prolotherapy, a much less invasive procedure. Insurance companies considered prolotherapy to be "non-traditional" and "experimental/investigative." No doubt, that was the case, as regenerative medicine was not yet out of the closet. For four years, we experimented with dozens of prolotherapy treatments, hoping that this would stabilize this major weight-bearing joint. Though this investment was profitable, it too was a temporary fix; the benefits only lasted for weeks. It did prove that when Kerri's sacroiliac joint was stable, she could live a normal, productive, and pain-free life.

Twelve years of experimentation and investigation, now affecting both of her sacroiliac joints, has now shown us our next step. These SI joints need stabilizing. We have also investigated the process of SI stabilization. We have learned that the fusion must be aligned correctly during the surgery.

This has been the secret to Dr. Lippitt's success. Vicki Sims, a physical therapist, goes into the operating room to ensure proper alignment during the procedure. He has a proven track record.

We have done everything to avoid surgery, as it is our last option. There are no other alternatives; my wife needs her sacroiliac joints fused. You have received letters from numerous medical professionals that have worked with Kerri for years, stating that this is a need. Please do not turn a deaf ear to them; please reconsider.

Sincerely,

Tim Shepherd

The Pennsylvania Department of Health Bureau of Managed Care received a request for a third level grievance appeal from me on January 7, 2004. Submitting the Certified Review Entity application for an external and independent review, we were assigned to the National Medical Review Board.

I asked Vince, my physical therapist; Dwight, my chiropractor; my prolotherapist; and family doctor, all of whom served me well for several years, to kindly provide a write-up of their experience with me and my health condition. All of them complied. It was apparent from reading the verdict from the Pennsylvania Department of Health that those who judged my case actually read the reports that my healthcare providers submitted. Those reviewing my case would not allow our insurance company to bow out of this. We won!

Finally, a year after meeting with Dr. Lippitt, I was scheduled for this surgery. Three days before we left for Atlanta, I got another call from our insurance company. The worker assigned to my case informed me that they were only required to pay 80% of what Medicare would cover, not 80% of the actual surgery cost. I kept thinking that if I could just have this surgery and it was successful, I would get a job and gladly pay the whole bill myself! It wasn't about the money; it was about escaping the pain. But I didn't tell the representative this. I would rather clean public toilets than have the job of telling clients that they won't have coverage for a surgery that they desperately need.

Grateful that we would get coverage for most of the surgery, we traveled to Georgia and settled into a very nice guesthouse for out-of-town patients, just blocks away from Emory Hospital in downtown Atlanta.

I couldn't have imagined a better hospital experience. Mrs. Sims was there to align me before and during my surgery. Patients like me can sublux easily from muscle spasms or simply from being moved from a gurney to the operating table. Dr. Lippitt drove two cannulated screws from both ilium into the sacrum and performed a bone graft in both joint spaces. Finally, I'd had the double sacroiliac fusion. Just telling you this makes me want to stand and sing Handel's "Hallelujah Chorus"!

Back home, I was so impressed with how well my muscles were responding. There was a lot of strengthening and balancing to work on, but it was *incredibly* encouraging to make continual progress. With stability, this was a whole different ball game. The only restrictions I had been given were no sky-diving or bungee jumping. No problem!

Six months after the surgery, I felt like I was twenty again, at least what I think I felt like when I was twenty. We had prayed for this for years! The SI fusions enabled me to live, not just exist. That for which I had all but given up hope was now my reality.

Although it was thirteen very difficult years to get resolution, I tried to just be thankful that I didn't have to wait another thirteen years for restoration. Unfortunately, my saga had many more chapters of unexplained pain.

A Closer Look at the UNCHANGING ONE

For all my life I have believed that God is good and that He loves me profoundly. However, in the dark pit of my despair, I doubted. I felt like the object of His wrath. The way in which I perceived God oscillated because of my fluctuating feelings and changing brain chemistry, but His nature is unchanging.

Unlike me, the Eternal One is dependable and consistent. His plans, promises, and purposes are never altered. God can't learn something new; He has complete knowledge. He does not develop or wane. For God to change would either make Him better or worse. That can't happen because He is a complete and perfect whole being.

Intense suffering will bring doubts and fears to the surface, but that doesn't alter who God is or the promises He has made. Though the world around me seems to be changing fast, as well as my aging body, God is the one constant in my life. I gather courage from that, knowing that the God of the Old and New Testaments is the same God at work in my life. His unfailing love, perpetual mercy, endless grace, and eternal power are mighty to save me too, from all that would discourage, depress, and destroy me.

CHAPTER 5

How Quickly Things Change
2004-2011

Life had radically changed. After so many years of counting ceiling tiles and such, you can imagine how happy I was to be free from the tyranny of pain. No longer undependable and restricted, I jumped into life with both feet and took on more and more responsibilities. I got involved with many good causes, but in six months I found myself overcommitted. The fact that I *could* be involved in almost anything didn't mean I *should* be. Well aware of physical limitations, I was learning that my emotional stamina and mental energy have limits as well. My treasured family was getting my leftovers. I needed to rein back and realign my priorities. It took time and energy to care well for my top God-given priorities of wife and mother. While our kids were now all quite independent teenagers and didn't seem to need me much, wholesome family relationships require time, focused energy, and devotion, no matter what the ages of our children — there are no substitutes.

There wasn't a day that passed that I didn't remember with gratitude the pain and restrictions from which I had been delivered. Honestly though, I felt robbed of what pain had stolen from me in those childrearing years. I'd never get those years back with my kids. I'd wanted to be consistent in my parenting, but the only thing consistent in my life had been pain. I wasn't as attentive to the needs of my kids as I should have been. Pain overshadowed everything, making vigilance difficult. Without health or money, I regretted not being able to do special things such as family outings and vacations. And I felt awful that I was such a drain on the family finances.

Thankfully, God prompted me to scrutinize these thoughts in the light of His truth. Because of my pain and debilitation, perhaps our kids became more compassionate for the weak and wounded of this world. No doubt, learning to serve me rather than be served by me helped build their character. We really did have both quantity and quality family time, even without the outings and family vacations. And God used other people in their lives to help fill in the gaps. I always had so much to be thankful for every day and in every stage of life. Perspective is always worth fighting for!

In 2005, there were a lot of changes for our family: Jessica got married in May, Jonathan left for college in August, and Julie began high school at home in September. Where had the time gone? I had just gotten my health back, and now my kids were leaving home. I wanted to turn the clock back and do it all over again with health! There was yet another significant change for us that summer: we moved.

The organization that we were part of in Venezuela asked us to consider being reinstated and join the staff at one of their training centers, located just twenty minutes away. They invited Tim to serve in construction and maintenance. Being a jack-of-all-trades man, he was an excellent match for this facility. We had prayed about this decision for a few months before taking this leap of faith. (In this organization, we never received a salary; instead, we were supported solely by donations.)

Our first year at this center ended up being their last year for teaching missionary candidates. The following year the campus underwent a big transformation. It was now open to groups of college students, teens, and adults to attend a new program called *Wayumi*. (This is a word derived from a Venezuelan Yanomami language which means *to go away for a short period of time for a specific purpose*.) This new program was designed to help people discover in a retreat atmosphere some of the whys and hows of cross-cultural missionary efforts to developing nations. I love physical work, and there was plenty of it on this 100-acre campus.

"Wonder Woman" was my new nickname; I think because it was a wonder that I could do so many things after suffering like I did for so many years. I knew that if my fusion were to break, I would plummet back into my old pain pattern. But now I knew where to go for help, so things would never get as bad as they had before — or so I thought.

In May of 2007, Tim and a small group of men left for Papua New Guinea (PNG). Their mission was to build a home for our friends on the island of New Ireland, north of the mainland. He came home from that trip all charged up to return — as in move there!

Just as military branches need personnel to serve the frontline troops, so missionaries working on the frontlines need people to help them in various support roles. While Tim was in PNG, he heard of many vacancies where there was a need for support personnel. A couple of those vacancies seemed suitable for us, so he became very excited about moving into one of those roles. Over the next several months, Tim's enthusiasm to move to PNG started to annoy me. I asked him to please stop talking about it for a while, since we already knew we wouldn't go for at least two years. So, Tim agreed to put this on the back burner.

A few weeks after Tim returned from PNG, we had the privilege of becoming grandparents. I'd never understood the half of its grandeur. I was right outside the door listening for Gabriel's first cry. I soon received that precious babe into my arms and into my heart forever! I didn't know what this new role of grandparenting was to look like, but I sure welcomed this new stage of life. It's a "high" that I have yet to come down from!

In February of 2008, our co-workers tragically lost their precious 18-year-old daughter to cancer. What a grievous time! She, who was so vivacious, outgoing, and joyful, was now gone from us. I was to serve dinner for the family the night before her funeral. As I headed down a few steps with a gallon of iced tea in each hand, both feet went out from under me. There was no opportunity to break my fall, but I did veer ever so slightly to the right, trying to avoid a direct blow to the buttocks. I managed to get my phone from my pocket but, because of my trembling, I was unable to call for help. I was embarrassed to be found by the family like this in their time of grief.

Before the paramedics moved me, they pushed around on various places to ascertain the injury site and discern the best way to move me. When they pushed on the kidney area, my pain went through the roof. At the hospital, the X-rays determined that nothing was broken. Thankfully, six weeks later, I was pretty much back to normal.

Although I had X-rays that looked good, I had a nagging hunch that something just wasn't right. I started having back spasms again. These intermittent flare-ups weren't nearly as severe as the previous ones, but they still put me completely down. Months later, I was more convinced that my right fusion had broken and only the pins in there were giving me connection. A year after my fall, I asked my doctor if he would look into this. He ordered X-rays, which confirmed that everything was intact. I remember sitting there in his office, somewhat shocked. How could everything be normal? Why does everything always look so good, yet not function? Most people with back pain are usually down for just two or three days. Not me. Why do I have such extensive flare-ups?

Over the next couple of years, I continued having significant back problems. I wasn't as debilitated as in the past, but I would be bedridden for three weeks and then spend another three weeks taking baby steps to become functional again. Given my past, I didn't think that being incapacitated for three weeks was that bad, but I sure didn't like it!

In the summer of 2008, both our daughter and our son got engaged to their loves. I was happy for them both initially, but soon after, I became depressed. The dreaded "empty nest" was upon me, and I hadn't prepared myself for this. Some parents long for this time in their lives. What was wrong with me? Being a mom was a hand-in-glove match, and I didn't want to take the glove off. I apologized to Jonathan and Julie many times for my tears. I felt so selfish. I wanted to be happy for them and with them, but I couldn't see this as anything but an end to our family. Tim didn't see things the same way. He said more than once, "Kerri, you act like you're falling off a cliff; this is just the next step." As logical as that was in my mind, my heart wasn't buying it. I *was* falling off a cliff!

I believe some of my tears were from the grief of having to raise my kids under the havoc and dysfunction of chronic pain. I got my health back just in time to watch my kids leave home. I really wanted to do this all over again — but with my health. I thought I would've been able to do a better job.

In this confusing time, I decided to do something that had helped me in that dank, dark, horrible depression in 1996. I grabbed a piece of paper and made two lists. I contrasted how I was feeling, the subjective, with the facts, the objective. It was helpful to hold my feelings up to the light of truth and take a good hard look. Doing this helped remind me of how dangerous it is to live by my feelings, which are subject to many variables. Though it felt wrong that our family was breaking up, it would not be best for them to remain under our roof. I realized that as adults, when my children come to me, it's not because they need me but because they want to be with me. This simple writing exercise also revealed that I was hanging more of my identity on being a mom than on being a child of the one true God.

Looking back over my life, it amazes me that God has used such an insecure situation (a misunderstood and debilitating health issue) to rescue me from my feelings of "not enoughness" and to make me a much more secure individual.

As a kid, there were many things I didn't understand, but I didn't ask questions because I thought I was supposed to already be in the know, and I didn't want to look stupid. I often compared myself with my older brothers and found myself coming up short. As a student, I struggled with reading. I could read the words and analyze the parts of speech, but I had an awful time trying to comprehend what those words were saying. In my senior year of high school, I had room in my schedule for a reading course, which thankfully helped me get on track. But by then I was already convinced that since there was so much reading in college, I would never survive. I believed I wasn't smart enough.

Fresh new insecurities of my "not enoughness" accompanied my thrill of becoming a mother. Parenting was an enormous responsibility. The closer I got to my due date, the more nightmares I had of being an incompetent mother. Then motherhood unraveled during my personal great depression. It took roughly two years for me to recover emotionally from that mental illness. By then, I had teenagers, moody people who would challenge my authority and outwit me. I had lost my "mom moorings." There were some times when I thought I was doing a decent job, but mostly I felt like I wasn't the mom my kids needed. Then I fell apart when my kids left home, and I wasn't enough without them.

As chronic debilitation invaded my life, it seemed to increase the rub. Pain seared, limitations mounted, schedules got scrapped, careers crashed, and dreams were dashed; pervasive affliction threatened to pull me under. I had no ability to make dinner, much less "make something of myself." I certainly was not enough to deal with all of the pain and loss.

Although no one ever sat me down and told me that my self-worth came from what I could accomplish, I was surrounded by that philosophy. Personally, I found a lot of satisfaction and happiness from physical work and serving other people. Then, for nearly three decades, God took away, or greatly restricted, my ability to function.

The subliminal message from the world around me is loud and clear: self-worth comes from a position, a pretty face, a paycheck, or popularity. Clever marketing strategies target insecurities and try to convince me that whatever they are selling will fix my "not enoughness." Everything surrounding me is continually changing or subject to change: the economy, friendships, health, homestead, occupation, people's opinions, and perspectives. All these pseudo-securities are shifting sand. Significance derived from anything that can be tainted, changed, or removed is in jeopardy.

Does the significance of my life wax and wane when I know more, read better, have children to raise, have an empty nest, or am confined to bed? It can seem that way. The fact that I struggled with my identity was proof that I wrestled with deceptive thinking. The truth is, our lives are *always* significant and meaningful, even when they don't feel like it. I need an objective standard that will never be changed or taken away.

I've found that objective standard in the Bible, which tells me that I've been made by God and for God. Because of that, He is rightly qualified to set the standard by which I measure my value. God said that He made me in His image, His likeness. When I laugh and cry, think and reason, create and relate, I am mirroring something of His character. And God's immense love for His image bearers gives us inestimable worth. Being highly treasured by the Almighty is to be esteemed as the pinnacle of significance. These two things are the core of our relevance as people. Absolutely nothing can alter or remove that favor. God's perspective is accurate, trustworthy, and eternal.

Measuring sticks vary, and people-pleasing is exhausting. However, living for an audience of One, God, is freeing and life-giving. No matter how broken, stripped, or messed up I am, the truth is that nothing will prevent me from being a treasured image bearer of the God of the Universe. When my significance is firmly rooted in God's opinion, I'll always have an accurate selfie.

In the shifting sand of affliction, it's a privilege to be anchored to truth. But learning to esteem God's opinion over mine or anyone else's is an ongoing battle that I'll fight until I meet my Maker. Since it's so easy to buy into lies, I need to continually rehearse what is truth in my mind. Contending for truth is always worth the fight.

As anticipated, 2009 held yet more changes for our family. On a chilly but sunny Saturday, one week before Valentine's Day, Tim walked our elegantly beautiful Julie down the aisle to marry Billy, her one and only love. She moved to New Jersey, where her husband was employed. The next month we welcomed Jessica's second little one, our creative Tyler, into our family; another grandson to love! She was now a busy momma of two, living three hours away in upstate New York. Then in May, Jonathan graduated from university. Three weeks later, Tim had the honor of officiating the marriage ceremony of Jonathan and his beautiful bride, Jolie. They moved to the suburbs of Philadelphia.

Just like that, we were empty nesters. Thankfully, two months before the first wedding, my waterworks had stopped; I had no more sorrow. That's how it is with God's grace. He gives His children the help and comfort when needed but not for the anticipation of the need.

Eight weeks after Jon and Jolie's wedding, I had another significant flare-up. Although I was doing all I knew to do, I saw no improvement for weeks on end. Locally, I wasn't getting the help I needed, so I decided to have a conference call with Mrs. Sims in Georgia, the SIJD specialist. She recommended a Medrol Dose pack of steroids, which thankfully turned me around. Over-the-counter medication never touched my pain and narcotics didn't do enough. They were working to block intense pain, whereas the steroids were reducing the inflammation that caused the pain.

The flare-up reminded me that I'm never in charge of my health. I can do all that I know to do to be healthy, but that doesn't guarantee a thing. Contrary to what my culture would have me believe, I'm not autonomous. Though I have no control over what happens to me, I do, however, always have control of my attitude and reactions. But what was God's purpose in all of this? I sure didn't understand why I was having such significant back problems again, but I acknowledged that my sovereign God did, and I needed to trust Him.

It had been two years since Tim had been to Papua New Guinea, and the idea of serving there was still pulling at his heartstrings. We got the boost we needed when our good friends offered us their frequent flyer miles to take a survey trip to PNG. We took our marathon journey to the other side of the world in January of 2010.

When we returned home from our survey trip, we began to seek counsel and input about moving overseas. First and foremost, we wanted the honest opinions of our children. We needed to know whether they were on board with our moving to PNG or not. We also talked with extended family, co-workers, and church leadership. Everyone gave us their blessing to go and affirmed that the job as "house parents" at the boarding school was a good match for us. Having received all green lights, we made our interests known to our organization's administration in the USA and PNG.

Though we were making plans to move to the other side of the world to serve the children of missionaries, it came with a high price tag. It was made all too real as I was with Julie and Billy that wonderful spring day in 2010 when our first beautiful granddaughter, Riley, entered this world. My heart was captivated with love for this newest member of our family. However, pain stabbed at my heart when I allowed myself to think about not being there to be a part of her growing-up years. It wasn't moving halfway around the world to live in a developing nation with a brand-new language that I wrestled with; it was leaving our three grandkids.

In September, we drove to Wisconsin for training. Unfortunately, before we left on this trip, I started having some trouble with my back. However, I was still able to attend the sessions and avoid a catastrophe.

A few weeks later, we finally took a family vacation. We got a killer deal on a large house in the Outer Banks of North Carolina and had a wonderful time. Sadly, the trip home took a toll on my back, and I encountered catastrophic pain. I spent the next three weeks in bed. No sooner had I gotten back on my feet when I was knocked down again for another three weeks. I was now concerned about being able to recover in time to get to PNG in January, as planned. Some self-induced pressure was relieved when my physical therapist said that we should move our departure date further ahead. Healing has its own timetable; mine sure seemed to be longer than most.

By now, I had a growing suspicion that my back was not up for this new adventure we were embarking on. But I didn't want to use that card as an excuse. If this fusion was intact, why was I having so much difficulty again? I expressed my concerns to the personnel responsible for our houseparent training, because going into this, I wanted no surprises for anyone. They didn't see it as a problem. Tim and I talked about this several times. Ever the optimist, he continued to reassure me that since he would have no other responsibilities placed on him, he could care for both the teens in the house and me. Besides, it was culturally normal to employ nationals to come six days a week to help with things like food preparation, cleaning, and laundry.

One day after physical therapy and just a few weeks away from leaving for Papua New Guinea, I headed down our rather steep stairs. My legs buckled from having worked them pretty hard in physical therapy that morning, and I fell to the bottom. As I sat there shaken, but completely unharmed, I said to God, "I know that we are *only* going to end up in PNG if You want us there." He knew my heart: I didn't want to force this window open, nor was I trying to slam it shut. Tim and I both wanted to trust God to put us where He wanted us. The confidence that it was God leading and enabling us to go PNG proved to be very comforting in the upcoming months.

I determined ahead of time that I was going to give myself wholly to this new opportunity. Though I was leaving those nearest and dearest to me back in the USA, I wanted to pour my heart and soul into these students and not hold back in any way. It's hard to describe the mixed emotions of a transition like this. I was nervously excited about serving in this venue.

Now at ages 47 and 49, seated on the plane as it prepared to leave the tarmac of a Chicago airport to fly halfway around the world, I contemplated our good-byes when we first moved overseas to Venezuela 25 years prior. In comparison, leaving our kids and grandkids was much harder! But it really was all right that my heart didn't agree with my mind because I had grace. Having experienced God's amazing grace time and time again, I had confidence that it would be sufficient for what we were leaving behind and for what lay ahead.

A Closer Look at the HIGHEST ROYAL RULER

God's rightful royal authority impacts my identity. He made me, so His opinion is the only accurate opinion that matters; I am who He says I am. How foolish of me to allow someone else to define me; especially when they aren't in charge.

God has supreme authority over all things. He doesn't cause evil to happen, but He allows it because He gave man the ability to make choices. His sovereignty is in harmony with man's free will and human responsibility, though I can't seem to iron out all those wrinkles.

God rules in righteousness. He is the highest. He answers to no one and owes no one an explanation. When God sovereignly speaks, things happen. Nothing can thwart God from accomplishing His ultimate good plan. Knowing that God's sovereignty is enveloped by his merciful compassion, goodness, faithfulness, and love, I conclude that rebelling against His will will never take me to a better place.

When God sovereignly chooses to hold off healing, it is according to His good, merciful, and loving plan for me. I can't begin to make sense of the backside of the tapestry of life, with all its muddled-up mess of tangled strings, but I know God is at work, weaving something beautiful on the other side. My responsibility is to cooperate with Him and let Him have control of that needle. No one and no situation can prevail against His purpose for my life, even if I can't interpret it as good, merciful, or loving.

CHAPTER 6

Déjà vu
2011

"We are not necessarily doubting that God will do the best for us; we are wondering how painful the best will turn out to be."[9] *C.S. Lewis*[7]

We arrived in the beautiful country of Papua New Guinea, the *Land of the Unexpected*, weary to the bone. I should have listened to my body and gone straight to bed. But the people around us encouraged us to stay up until nightfall to get our internal clocks turned around.

Our fourth day in the country, we walked to the top of a steep hill to join a couple who had invited us for dinner. During the meal, the pain I knew so well crept over me. *Oh no! I can't sit up anymore*, I thought. *Just endure. Tough it out. Soon you can go to bed.* But truth be told, I felt like I couldn't possibly remain seated through the next five minutes! I was trying to avoid drawing attention to myself, but when I broke out into a cold sweat, Tim noticed. My pain increased so rapidly that I quickly became the center of attention. I didn't want to expose my back pain any more than I would want to expose a hemorrhoid. My unexplained sudden pain was personal.

That was the beginning of four months of debilitating pain, where I was mostly bedridden. Some of those weeks, I was completely bedridden apart from going to the bathroom. Other weeks I could be up for a total of an hour throughout the day. I tried so hard to get back on my feet, appropriating everything that we had learned over the years. It was so discouraging, frustrating, confusing, and lonely. I had come to PNG, determined to dig into new friendships, but who would want to darken the door of a suffering stranger.

This analogy came to me in the middle of a wicked flare-up in the '90s. It gives symbolism to the major flare-ups I've had. Imagine being alone in a dark jungle, struggling to survive. Fear and vulnerability are your only companions. To get to the "land of the living" where people enjoy life, you must cross a murky river. You have no watercraft, tools, or weapons. But what you do have is the ability to swim and the desire to get to the good land. Into the water you go, excited to join the others. Not far into your swim, an alligator snags, chews, and spews you back onshore where you started. There you lie, gravely wounded, incredibly weak, and devastated. You receive rations and encouragement, and you heal — ever so slowly. A couple of months later, you've recovered. You step into the river again, hoping to reach the other side. This time, you poignantly understand the risks, because you know the alligator is still in there. This time you make it halfway across before you are again snagged, chewed, and spewed. Does it matter that you made it a little farther this time? No, because the results were the same. You will continue to try, hoping that somehow, someday, you'll reach the other side. You don't know how many times it will take until you reach the land of the living or if you will survive the next attack.

Spring of 2011

Dear God,

Oh, how this flare-up stirs my memories. Just like a fragrance or song can take me to bygone days, this level of pain ushers in a whole mess of ugly memories. This utter weakness causes me to wonder how I ever made it through the dire straits of previous years. It makes me marvel at Your grace. Obviously, You carried me. You gave me the ability to endure when my strength and desire ran out. Will You please hold me again? I know You are faithful!

Kerri

In our minds, taking steroid medication was pulling out the big guns. Yet further down the road, an orthopedic explained to me that it was more beneficial to take steroids than to lie in bed for weeks on end. How I wish I had known that sooner. I was so disappointed that the steroids gave me no relief this time. And I was kicking myself for not bringing my TENS unit.

Acquiring medications turned out to quite burdensome because there were so few available. Tim went to town and visited the pharmacies to see what he could locate and returned terribly disappointed. They had none of the medications he was looking for nor anything close to it.

A sense of déjà vu washed over me. I felt a bitter, sick feeling in the pit of my stomach. That "stuck-and-sunk" feeling I had back in Venezuela returned. Once again, the available pain medication was just not strong enough. How could this possibly be happening to me again? *This is pitiful,* I thought. *Another living nightmare!* When I could drag my thoughts away from myself, I wondered, *what do these dear people here in PNG do when they are in serious pain?*

Then I remembered a scene from our survey trip last year over in the island region of the country. An elderly villager was showing us his impressive pineapple patch. And there, among the pineapples, were flourishing marijuana plants. When I saw the plant in this context, it suddenly dawned on me that God created this stuff and called it good! (Genesis 1:11, 12). Up until that point, I had only ever thought of it as something harmful. It seems to me that mankind is very adept at spoiling every good gift God has given us. (In case you're wondering, I didn't use it, but I was desperately considering all options.)

Each month that passed, we expected to see this flare-up fade; but this wasn't my typical "three weeks down, three weeks getting back on my feet" ordeal. Because the pain didn't let up, we were not able to step into the boarding house and care for the students when school began in August. This weighed heavily on our hearts because it meant an unexpected change for another couple to fill the vacancy we left.

After fifteen weeks, the worst pain finally subsided. I was able to begin the mental work of language learning, which served as a great distraction from pain and limitation. It's expected of us "newbies" to the country to learn the Melanesian pidgin language in the context of their cultural community. Tim followed his language helper throughout the day, harvesting and drying coffee beans, wrapping bananas, fishing, laying-up a thatched roof, and making fire without matches. Because I was unable to go to the village, we hired a local woman to come to our apartment to help me learn the language.

The first couple of days that my language helper, Junio, came, she pulled up a chair beside my bed and sat with me. She would say something to me, and of course, I had no idea what she was saying. She was kind and patient. But when she left, I cried. This wasn't working. I had no idea how I was going to learn this language. Tim and I prayed about what to do. I believe God gave me the idea to study biblical narratives with her since she knew and loved her Bible. Even though we were from extremely different worlds, our mutual love for Jesus drew us close. Our four hours together flew by quickly when I grew in my ability to speak and to understand. I looked forward to hearing her sweet singsong *"mow-ning"* as she approached our door. We read the Bible and prayed together, told stories from our past, and laughed a lot. Her friendship was the perfect antidote for the loneliness I felt.

There was only one time that she did not greet me with a huge smile. Junio had come in the afternoon, which was odd as well. She relayed to me that her house, a grass hut, had just been robbed. The member of her clan, who stayed behind to guard the families' homes and belongings, was held at knifepoint. When threatened, her family member quickly fled.

She told me that she had lost everything: her clothes, oil lamp, matches, blankets, pot, and cups were all gone. What worried her the most was her inhaler, which she couldn't live without. I walked with her to the doctor's office on the base and assured her that she would get another one. As we sat in the office waiting, I just didn't know what to say to comfort her. I could hardly get over the fact that she listed her matches as something that was stolen. When I told her that I would give her some of my clothes, she added, "And when I'd stand up, they'd fall down!" Somehow, we always managed a good laugh.

Junio has lived a very hard life. Her suffering, very different from mine, has been significant in many different ways. Her clan and countrymen have suffered from a lack of what most of us would consider the bare necessities. Every day I would spend some time lying on the floor of our porch, watching citizens walk up and down the road. This helped my perspective, as I didn't feel so alone. Life was very hard for them too. Yet, they smiled. I don't think they shared my disappointment, as their expectations weren't so high. As an American, I have such high expectations: I expect three meals a day, safety, perfection in products, a comfortable living environment, respect from others, excellence in healthcare, and a relatively pain-free life. With such high expectations, no wonder I get so disappointed. Oh, to live with expectancy but not expectation!

While living in Papua New Guinea, I discovered the fascinating book, *Pain, the Gift Nobody Wants*. The author, Dr. Paul Brand, says, "On my travels, I have observed an ironic law of reversal at work: as a society gains the ability to limit suffering, it loses the ability to cope with what suffering remains. ... Certainly, the 'less advanced' societies do not fear physical pain as much. I have watched Ethiopians sit calmly, with no anesthetic, as a dentist works his forceps back and forth around a decaying tooth. Women in Africa often deliver their babies without the use of drugs and with no sign of fear or anxiety. These traditional cultures may lack modern analgesics, but their beliefs and family support systems built into everyday life help equip individuals to cope with pain. The average Indian village knows suffering, expects it, and accepts it as an unavoidable challenge of life. Their attitude makes a difference. In a remarkable way, the people of India have learned to control pain at the level of the mind and spirit and have developed endurance that we in the West find hard to understand. Westerners, in contrast, tend to view suffering as an injustice or failure, an infringement on their guaranteed right to happiness."[10]

Before I read this book, I could only see pain as my enemy. But after listening to some of his experiences and lessons learned from his forty plus years of working with the leprous community, I've come to understand that pain protects us from destroying ourselves. Dr. Brand calls pain, "the loyal scout announcing the enemy." He says that "every bodily activity that we view with irritation or disgust — blisters, calluses, fever, sneezes, coughs, vomiting, and pain — is an emblem of the body's self-protection."[11]

My perspective always needs recalibrating. I have so much to be thankful for every day and in every circumstance of life.

Over the next several weeks I found that I could be up for a couple of hours each day. I made the most of that time getting to know the people around me. Eventually, I had a little job in the finance office that took about three or four hours each week, managing petty cash and currency from different countries.

Apart from my issues, Tim was really enjoying his time in PNG. I encouraged him to be out and about, to get involved with people and activities. Being adept with tools of all kinds, he began to work on maintenance projects on the missionary base. When school started in August, he taught a daily Bible class, a high school Phys-Ed class, and woodshop classes for high school students. Maintenance now became his part-time job.

I was still very suspicious of a broken right SI fusion. Tim argued that even if the fusion broke, the pins would prevent subluxation from happening. But if that were true, I wondered why my ankles weren't aligned.

Before my fusion surgery, I would check my alignment by sitting with my back up against a wall and with my legs straight out in front of me. My right ankle bone was almost always higher than my left ankle bone. To correct this, I would lie down and have Tim pull my right leg downward until my ankle bones were even with one another. Misaligned ankles were always a sign that my SI joint wasn't in place.

So why did aligning that right SI joint relieve my pain if the fusion was intact? Tim thought something else must be wrong or that I had this pain because I was getting older. It was true, I was getting older, but most people forty years older than me could stand for five or ten minutes without getting into trouble. In those days I needed Tim to pull down on that right leg all the time to reduce my pain, just like before my fusion. If it wasn't the SI joint, I couldn't imagine what it would be. There were too many parallels to my experience years ago.

Standing was the worst. For that reason, I tried to avoid people when Tim wasn't with me. I didn't want to be rude and walk away from someone when they stopped to meet or greet me, nor did I want to suffer more weeks in bed just because I stood three minutes too long to speak with someone. Tim was ever my protector, inviting people to walk with us, or quickly getting me to a supportive chair.

When I was well enough, Tim and I would take evening walks around the tennis and basketball courts, a stone's throw away from our apartment. These walks were very controlled and never increased by more than one lap around. Sometimes during these walks, my back would suddenly go into spasm. We would stop right away to check my alignment, and sure enough, it was askew. Since my same symptoms were back, didn't it stand to reason that the problem be a broken fusion?

As we began to see the need to return to America, the big question that loomed over our heads was, "How are we ever going to get back to America?"

I tried to strengthen my core muscles, but like before, exercise wasn't cutting it. I could only get a little strength built up before re-injury would occur. If you've ever needed to exercise a joint that continued to dislocate, you understand. If only I'd had my sacroiliac belt and TENS unit.

After a few more scary flare-ups during the school year, Tim told me that he couldn't stand the pressure of trying to focus on teaching at the school when he didn't know what condition I was in at home. He decided that we would not finish out the school year but leave as soon as I could fly. We departed two months later.

We had talked to a doctor who had just returned from the United States about going on steroids for our trip home. His advice was that I begin the steroid treatment a week before our departure and finish them up on our journey home. Targeting the inflammation before the trip started was fantastic advice. Due to the steroids, the inflammation aggravated by the trip was minimal compared to what it would've been without them.

Purchasing tickets was somewhat of a gamble. Since I had little stamina, we booked six flights and reserved five hotel rooms for the journey home. Tim rolled up a yoga mat and attached it to the outside of a carry-on because I had to lie down all along the way. Since Hawaii was our halfway point, we spent three nights there so I could better rest up for the second leg of the journey. The flight from Hawaii to Seattle was the worst for two reasons: it was the only flight where I couldn't lie down, and it was also an extremely turbulent flight.

After I started doing the Lamaze breathing to help me bear the pain, we decided we needed to ask the flight attendants to please clear out of the back of the plane, so that I could lie down and have Tim align me. Unfortunately, the alignment didn't hold because the muscles were in a great spasm. I thought I had taken the maximum dose of the prescription narcotic, only to find out later that I could have safely taken twice the amount. Ugh!

Our time in Papua New Guinea may have looked like a failure since we didn't do what we intended, but we can look back and see

God's faithfulness in hardship as well as a few good things that happened that year through our connections with students, staff, and nationals. But is success defined by what we accomplish? Thankfully, God's economy is vastly different from ours. Perhaps we "accomplished" all that God intended that year. I believe that learning to trust Him more deeply in the tough times *is* success in God's eyes.

A Closer Look at the FAITHFUL ONE

I see God's faithfulness everywhere: sustaining our planet in the Milky Way, the precision of each sunrise and sunset, the seasons, the creatures and critters, and the food on my plate! How can we not see His faithfulness? God is not a wishy-washy Father, in a good mood one minute and ticked off the next. No, He acts according to His character. And what a gift that my faithlessness doesn't nullify His faithfulness!

When circumstances are bleak and God's faithfulness seems more like abandonment, it's time for me to step back and look at the big picture of what I *can* see that God has already accomplished. Doing this builds my confidence to trust His faithfulness over my feelings.

Reading through the Old Testament Scriptures, I witness God's faithfulness to the Israelite nation for thousands of years. He never abandoned a mission or left a loose end. His love and faithfulness to them was demonstrated by keeping every promise He made to them.

The "scarlet thread" interwoven from Genesis through Revelation reveals God's faithfulness to His magnificent plan to redeem the whole human race. Those who truly trust in God never do so in vain. His faithfulness continues to all generations, even mine! Reminiscing on His faithfulness in the past encourages me to trust Him when the next crisis hits.

CHAPTER 7

So Close and Yet So Far

FEB 2012 – FEB 2013

It was so good to reunite with our family! We quickly found winter clothing and settled into a tiny but furnished guestroom back on the campus we had left a year ago. Tim moved back into his maintenance and construction responsibilities right away. I, however, told the leadership that it would be a very long time until I was well enough to contribute in any way on the Wayumi campus. That certainly proved true!

Just weeks after we returned from Papua New Guinea, Julie gave birth to our fourth grandchild, a bundle of joy named Chloe! Riley would know the blessing of having a younger sister. That was something I'd always longed for — being the youngest with three older brothers. I'm thankful we weren't halfway around the world missing her grand entry. Being back in America gave me the privilege of loving and nurturing my grandchildren, which is a very special role for me!

My next anticipated event was to see Vicki Sims, the sacroiliac specialist in Georgia. But the insurance company's protocol postponed that until I had an appointment with our family doctor, another round of x-rays, and six weeks of physical therapy. Though being in America meant I was closer to getting help — significant help — it was still down the road. I was so close, and yet so far!

With memories of being insulted and marginalized, going to any new health care provider was always distressing. But Shari, a local physical therapist that specialized in pelvic problems, came highly recommended. Would she truly believe me or just listen politely and nod her head? When I was in pain, I could barely talk about my past without tears. At previous appointments, whenever I'd cry, it was assumed that I was depressed. Since my test results didn't warrant the amount of pain I *claimed* to have had, the typical conclusion was that my physical pain was magnified by depression. How would she interpret my tears? Here I was, worried about being stereotyped while I was stereotyping her!

I hardly knew where to begin when Shari asked, "What's wrong?" It seemed like such a simple question, but for me, it was quite loaded! Do I start with the last year or the previous twenty? What pertinent information could I give her in fifteen minutes? There was always so much room for misunderstanding when I saw someone new.

Right off the bat though, I liked her. She was very knowledgeable, instructive, professional, and personable. After the physical evaluation, she said, "I understand why you are in bed all the time; you have zero stability in your pelvis. Zero! You're just flip-flopping all around. It's going to be a long, hard road to recovery."

I told her that I was not afraid of hard work, as long as it moved me in the right direction. She advised me to walk with baby steps and to keep my knees together so as not to cause further injury. She gave me a new SI belt to wear and started me on simple exercises to start firing up my dormant pelvic muscles.

Shari and I ended up talking about counseling. She agreed that there was nowhere in our area that offered help for people living with chronic pain. And I wasn't in any physical condition to travel. Interestingly, she mentioned that it takes the brain a full year to recover from the types of flare-ups I had. So now I had a good excuse for my fuzzy mind!

Over the years I would forget the things that I learned in past flare-ups, so I began taking notes: *Advice to Self* I called it. *(See Appendix.)*

An orthopedic doctor across the hall from Shari suited me up with a back brace. Over the years, trial and error taught me how to use braces successfully. Pulling out of a significant flare-up was an excellent time to use it, because of severe weakness; but overuse of a brace hindered the strengthening of those weak muscles.

I was learning from Shari by leaps and bounds. One of the most important things I learned from her was that you could not tell from an x-ray if a joint was successfully fused. She said that I would need a CT scan for that. If I had only known that years ago.

A Journal Entry from April 18, 2012

It's the night before the results of my CT scan. I'm both nervous and excited about the results. I keep thinking that my right SI fusion has to be broken. I'm sure that's the problem, but Tim wants me to prepare for the fact that the scan may show nothing. He says, "If that's the case, we'll be ok. We'll keep pressing on for answers."

I love his optimism, most of the time. For the last several years, Tim has said that this problem is manageable. He stopped saying that in PNG. If the scan shows nothing, I could come home feeling hopeless. But in truth, I won't be hopeless. Perplexed, but not in despair.

I need to continually remind myself that my hope is not in a test, a surgery, medicine, or any doctor, but in the Lord God. My Great Physician knows what's wrong. And in His time, He can steer me to the help I need or could instantly heal me. There are no promises that I'll have healing on this earth, but I'm thankful that there is a time coming when I will no longer bear sin's curse in my body. Jesus will redeem this earth and make everything new, including me! I can't wait to live life to the fullest with no more consequences of sin: no more suffering, sickness, pain, grief, or death.

Do I need to be pain-free to be content? It seems that I need a measure of health to be able to sleep and eat, not in agonizing levels of pain or severe chemical imbalance. But do I need to walk out of that office tomorrow with a diagnosis? Just because I feel as I did in my pre-fusion days, it doesn't necessarily mean that that's what's wrong with me — although it sure seems like it to me. As much as I don't want to go through surgery again, I just can't fathom living like this. If only exercise could fix this.

Since success in God's eyes is learning to trust and depend on Him more, could it be that what God desires to teach me through suffering is more valuable for me than I could ever imagine? I want to live with expectancy, confident that God will sustain me and somehow use all of this for His good purposes. However, that takes more faith than I have at the moment. This is yet another wrestling match of truth versus feelings.

The CT report indicated a successful bone fusion on my left SI joint and a "not as conclusive" on my right side. It appeared there may have been some spots that were fused, but the screws were in the proper position. What was I to do with *that* information?

We were finally able to secure appointments with Vicki Sims and Dr. Weis, the new orthopedic surgeon partnering with Mrs. Sims. With previous surgery records transferred, plane tickets purchased, hotel and car rental reservations made, and current CT scan and x-rays in hand, we made our way to Georgia. I even had a tentative surgery date to re-fuse my right sacroiliac joint. Because of the fiasco that we had prior to the first fusion surgery, Tim had me call the insurance company again to confirm insurance coverage. For me, the excitement was mounting, but not for Tim. He kept saying, "This is moving along too easily. Something isn't right."

Our first stop in Georgia was to visit the neurologist in downtown Atlanta for piriformis testing, as we had done the last time. Then we drove an hour north to Gainesville Physical Therapy, an oasis where thousands who have long suffered from sacroiliac dysfunction finally received help. I was confident that I would get help here again. Although I knew Dr. Lippitt had retired, I assumed that I would still get another quick diagnosis like I did the last time, by simply moving my legs around. I was sure that I would soon be whisked away to the operating room to get this thing re-fused. Such expectations! In my opinion, this chapter of my life had gone on long enough, as it had now been five years since that nasty hard fall on my buttocks.

After listening carefully to my story, asking pertinent questions, and examining me, Mrs. Sims said that I had a disc problem. *What? No way! That's not my problem!* I argued back in my head.

Her conclusion rocked my boat! I had no sharp shooting pain down my leg. What about my subluxation? Of all things, I just happened to be correctly aligned when I saw her. Ugh! But it wouldn't have mattered anyway. On a subsequent visit, when I wasn't properly aligned, she told me that she believed that muscle spasms were pulling the whole right ilium up because subluxation couldn't happen with the screws in place. While I understood her logic, I was positive that subluxation was happening. And while it didn't make sense that I would sublux with screws in place, why, when Tim pulled on my leg, making my ankles even again, did that relieve the pain? I reasoned that somehow those screws were sliding back and forth in there.

What a quandary! Who was I to contradict her, the expert? I had been so sure that if I could just get to that place, the mecca for SIJD, I would get the help I needed. I was so sure that they would see things as I did. I was bewildered!

Mrs. Sims was so happy to tell me about a wonderful disc rehabilitation program called the Pettibon System. It had helped so many of her patients. She said it would take six months of rehabilitation, but that the results would be worth it. She assured me that I would be feeling much better in just a couple of weeks. A staff member could train me in the procedure the next day, and they could order everything I would need and have it sent to our home.

I kept my impending appointment with Dr. Weiss later that day. Foreboding thoughts invaded my mind as I lay on the floor in his waiting room a couple of hours later. Nausea hit as I struggled to hold back my tears. I felt further away than ever to getting this joint re-fused. I believed my Great Physician knew precisely what was going on inside of me. If I completely trusted God, why did it seem like my hope was now dangling by a thread again? Had I *still* not learned to trust Him? Being extremely disappointed and stressed was proof that I was wrestling, yet again, with trusting God.

I needed help to keep my eyes on Jesus and not the storm within. I needed to let the truths I had learned from God's Word speak to my anxious heart. He is in control of all things, and that includes my health. I strove to be proactive in this quest for help, but I couldn't pry open a locked door. I wanted to trust God to open the doors that needed to open and close the doors that needed to close. And I desired to trust His timing. But I was so weary of it all. Being in a personal relationship with God meant that I could honestly express all of my feelings to Him and freely confess my desperate need for His help to endure all of this. There was no need to pretend. God knew my thoughts before I could even put them into words. There was nothing about my circumstances that I could change except my perspective. Focusing on what I had to be thankful for helped me see that my life was rich and full. Yet the pain was relentless and crippling. I was truly at God's mercy, but aren't we all?

I figured Dr. Weiss's assessment would agree with Mrs. Sims's, which it did. Both doctors had pushed between the L4 and L5 vertebrae, inflicting pain. During my appointment, I had several questions for him, one of which was, "Can't you tell by examination that there is abnormal movement in the right SI joint?" That was how Dr. Lippitt had made my first SI diagnosis. He humbly responded, "I'm sorry, I'm just not that good yet." I hadn't meant any disrespect. I needed to remain calm and polite, but my growing angst longed for more satisfactory answers. I was trying to hide my despair.

I had to remind myself over and over that I was not the expert. These two have studied the human body for decades and have had experience with thousands of people with SIJD. They knew this dysfunction. However, I knew my body; I was the expert on me. I couldn't help but listen to what my body was telling me. Somehow, the professionals and I needed to get on the same page.

The next day, as I sat in the waiting room at Gainesville Physical Therapy, I read from two huge photo albums packed with note cards of appreciation to Mrs. Sims from her SIJD patients. My heart was overwhelmed from reading note after note; I had felt so alone in this journey. Now I was "meeting" my neighbors, other people who had lived in my neighborhood of pain, confusion, misunderstanding, and marginalization.

Later, in Vicki's consultation room, I sat contemplating the individuals those notecards represented — people whose lives witnessed personal destruction at the hand of SIJD: shattered families, finances, and hopes. I read mere snippets from the album, but Mrs. Sims had heard every one of their stories. Maybe someday my note of thanks would make it into one of her albums.

Mrs. Sims allowed Tim and me plenty of time to ask the questions we had written down the night before. She answered each one carefully, with patience, kindness, and intelligence. Her courteous manner was a welcome oasis. Could she possibly know what a blessing she was to so many?

Back home, parts of the equipment for the Pettibon System began to arrive. Tim went straight to work welding a contraption for pelvic traction, so we didn't have to buy one. I was skeptical but followed this prescribed six-month program to a tee. We had a wobble seat, neck traction, foam wedges, and rollers. Between the two programs, the one for my degenerative disc and the one for pelvic stabilization with Shari, I spent four hours every day rehabilitating. No problem, nothing else was competing for my time. I've never lacked the motivation to work at anything that would move me away from pain and toward function.

The Pettibon System helped a tiny bit, making some movements easier. But sadly, it did not touch my debilitating pain. My symptoms remained the same as before my fusion in 2004: relentless pain in the left lumbar which could only be helped by constant alignment and bed rest. I could plank for five minutes but only stand for two or three. Exercise offered no help.

My new symptom that I'd had now for over a year was knee pain. Often when I slept, I would dream that I was in pain and wake up crying from real knee pain. The crazy thing was that it didn't hurt when I used it. Understanding how things can progress, or should I say, regress, we sought help at the sports medicine center.

My iliotibial (IT) band was super tight, obviously not from running, as is the usual case. This tendon starts at the ilium, where I was unstable. At this appointment, I learned about the Graston Technique, a process of scraping or massaging with instrumentation. The goal was to break up and stretch restricted fascia tissue to promote healing by making that hard tissue soft and pliable again.

In this form of therapy, one should apply the phrase, "no pain, no gain." You can either pay a trained individual to inflict you, purchase the expensive tools and learn from YouTube how to use them yourself, or grab a Backnobber, rolling pin, or a hard plastic something and go at it yourself. The pain will tell you where your trouble spots are. Tim didn't like inflicting pain on me, but some of the angles were too hard for me to work on myself.

Through these many years, my dear husband has been a very loving and faithful caregiver. When I'm incapacitated, Tim suffers right along with me, serving my needs around the clock. And never once have I heard him complain about the medical bills and inconveniences.

He never resents helping me in the middle of the night, no matter how many times I wake him. Before I would crawl into bed, I'd have to check my alignment, so I didn't go to sleep misaligned. Often Tim had to get out of bed to realign me simply because I got up to use the bathroom. Some flare-ups were such that I couldn't cover myself with the blankets or stand long enough to get myself a drink, but Tim was always glad to serve me, lightening my burdens in any way possible. He has aligned me thousands of times over the years — at home, friend's homes, roadside rest stops, stores, restaurants, churches, hospitals, banks, airports, gas stations, schools, and anywhere else we went. Good thing I married a maintenance man, since I'm such high maintenance!

For years, I've said that this back issue is way too big for me to manage on my own. Therefore, when I need to decipher whether I am well enough to go somewhere or do something, we decide together. Tim helps me look at the bigger picture, back at what I've recently done and ahead to what may be around the corner.

I've grown to trust his judgment because I know he always wants what's best for me. He's always trying to protect me from further hurt and harm. He has faithfully kept his vow before God to have me "for better, for worse, for richer or poorer, in sickness and in health." Caring for me has not been an easy task, but it's one in which, by God's grace, he has excelled. And I am forever grateful.

Before my journey of back pain began, I had wanted Tim to show a token of his love by buying me a little something for my birthday, anniversary, or Christmas. He usually didn't think about it until the night before, but by then, the action seemed to me to be motivated by guilt. How different things are now! I'm so very secure in his committed, self-sacrificial love for me that I don't need a token. Because of that, I've told him over and over to never give me a holiday or birthday gift, though any other time would be fine.

From August through October of 2012, I kept a journal, just a line or two each day about what I did or tried to do and couldn't. This journal painted a more accurate view of what I was going through. It conveyed more than I could explain during an appointment. Sadly, in this day and age, professionals have no time allotted to read such a thing, but Mrs. Sims is a rare gem among professionals: she made time to peruse and respond to my journal. In a conference call, she said: "You're hardly functioning at all!" Now I knew she was getting a better picture of my dysfunction.

But there were high points, namely, our grandkids. They were like rays of sunshine bursting through on a cloudy day. They have filled our lives with more joy than we could have ever anticipated. Seven months after our granddaughter Chloe was born, our third grandson entered this world. I wasn't in good shape, but I was well enough to lie down in the van on the way to the hospital and to camp out on the floor of the waiting room throughout the wee hours of the night, awaiting his arrival. When Jonathan and Jolie's son, Carter, was finally born, my heart swelled; it was love at first sight!

Ten days later, I wrote the following letter to our kids.

October 26, 2012

Dear Family,

We know God answers prayer: sometimes His answer is "yes," sometimes it's "no," and sometimes it's "wait." After the letter I got today from Mrs. Sims, it's clear that our answer is still "wait." I was really hoping to get a surgery date for next month.

This news would've been easier to accept if I wasn't in so much pain right now. I've been in bed for the last six days, and I'm feeling bummed that I am getting weaker. Hopefully, this won't be as hard to pull out of as the major flare-ups I had last year in PNG.

It's been almost a year since I've been bedridden for weeks on end. That's something to really be thankful for. I'm also grateful for the abundance of medication on my nightstand because many people in this world have nothing to help them deal with their pain. I have so much!

The letter said that "Dr. Weiss is requesting further testing before making a recommendation for surgical intervention." He wants the diagnostic SI injection (a shot of Lidocaine into the center of my buttocks) and a discogram. My heart sank after I had read this. The diagnostic SI injection of Lidocaine will show him nothing since I have referred pain to the lumbar area, not the SI joint. I learned from YouTube what a discogram is. Fluid is pushed through a needle in my discs to see if it reproduces my pain. If my pain can't be reproduced, then the disc is not the main pain generator.

I'm frustrated, disappointed, and impatient. But it's always been difficult at every turn to get help for my pain. This just means more time, more hassle, more money, and more waiting.

What Satan means to use to destroy me, God intends to use to refine me. God commits to use this painful condition for my good and His glory. Focusing on the enormity of what I have is way more beneficial than fixating over what I don't have. Rehearsing truths encourages me. Looking back, I clearly see God's care for me throughout the years. Yet tonight I'm struggling for peace and perspective. I'm trying to keep my hope in Jesus and not in a doctor! I certainly ask God to use them, but my trust must be in Him.

Love you all,

Momma

The emotional battle was raging, making sleep difficult. When I have completely sleepless nights, there is little doubt that depression is rearing its ugly head again. I had weaned off my antidepressant medication a year ago. Several times over these many years, I had weaned off that medication only to have to go back on it when a catastrophic flare-up would strike. Thankfully, I responded well to an increased dose of my antidepressant and was soon sleeping again.

During these days of struggle, Tim decided to write the following letter to Dr. Weiss.

November 13, 2012

Dear Dr. Weiss,

I've debated for some time about writing to you on behalf of my wife, your patient, Kerri Shepherd. We often pray for you that you will have wisdom and discernment as you make decisions not only for my wife but also for all your patients.

Kerri has suffered for 20 years now with SI joint dysfunction. It took us 13 years to figure that out because she does not show the typical signs for SIJD. For example, she rarely experiences pain in the SI joint itself. All her pain is due to muscle spasms in the lower back, primarily on the left side, yet it was her right SI joint that continually needed to be adjusted, which was the only thing that brought relief to the spasm. It was only after years of chiropractic care, physical therapy, and Prolotherapy that we were able to confirm that immobilizing the SI joint was the answer.

In 2004 we traveled to Georgia to see Mrs. Sims and Dr. Lippitt for a double SI fusion. The procedure was 100% successful. After rehab, she was able to return to a normal life. She was entirely pain-free for more than three years.

In 2008 Kerri fell down some steps, landing very hard on the right side of her pelvis. The x-rays taken showed that there was no fracture and that everything was fine.

However, after this fall, she started to experience flare-ups again. As time passed, they became more frequent and more severe. During each flare-up, she would show the exact same symptoms as her pre-surgery days.

We were living in Papua New Guinea in 2011, and that year ended up being one big, long flare-up. We had very little help there. After returning home in February of 2012, we started pursuing help, believing that the fusion on the right side was not intact.

According to the orthopedic doctor, the CAT scan showed no bone growth across the right side like the left side. We believe that, although the screws are still in place on the right side, they are no longer holding the joint stable. We believe that her fall back in 2008 jarred the screws loose, and over time they have grown looser, allowing for more movement resulting in more frequent and intense flares.

Upon visiting you and Mrs. Sims in May of this year, you both felt that a disk was the problem and not the SI itself. Mrs. Sims prescribed the Pettibon system for six months. Kerri did the program faithfully and saw only slight improvement in some areas of movement. Her major weight-bearing difficulties persisted, apparent subluxation of the right SI, and resulting muscle spasm in the lower-left lumbar region.

An MRI was ordered and showed some abnormality in one disk, but as you stated in your report, it "appears to be secondary to the mechanical issues."

You felt that re-fusing the right SI was reasonable if it could be determined to be the pain generator. This is a problem because Kerri, using traditional testing for SIJD, has never shown that the SI is the issue.

Yesterday, we went to see a pain specialist in our area. Before he would concede to do the discogram that you are asking for, he required an examination. During his evaluation, he administered the Faber test. (He had Kerri lie on her back with her right leg bent. He placed her right ankle on her left knee. With one hand on her right hip and his other hand on her right bent knee, he pushed it down. If he *reproduced her pain, it meant that the SI joint was an issue.) It was obvious from Kerri's face that he was hurting her a great deal, but she was not able to pinpoint the exact location of the pain. He pushed harder. He then repeated the test on the other side with the same results. She could not pinpoint the pain's epicenter, so he concluded that the SI is not the pain generator. Kerri was in tremendous pain 15 min later and needed to be aligned before we left his office. In fact, she is still recovering from the effect of this test.*

The point being, this doctor was stressing the SI with no typical SI pain reproduced. However, within minutes the muscle spasms had reached a level of tremendous pain. This always has been the case with Kerri: subluxation in the SI, not resulting in pain in the SI, but muscle spasm in the lower lumbar. This pain management doctor ordered a bone scan. He said that if there is movement in the SI joint, the bone scan will show the bone's irritation from abnormal movement. We are hoping that he is right about what the scan will show. Is that your understanding? The scan is this Thursday, and we see him again five days later. We will have the results of the bone scan sent to your office.

You and Mrs. Sim have both said that based on Kerri's symptoms and her response to the Pettibon System, it seems reasonable that the SI joint could still have movement and that the iFuse Implant surgery is a viable solution. We are pushing for that; we'd like to have this procedure done as soon as is possible.

Thank you, Dr. Wiess, for considering all these things. We greatly need and appreciate your help.

Timothy C. Shepherd

The iFuse Implant System is a means of stabilizing the sacroiliac joint using titanium plugs with porous surfaces which encourage tight bony ingrowth. Their triangular shape minimizes the chance of SI rotation or micromotion. Typically, three implants are used in this procedure, meaning there will be nine surfaces of intertwined bone growth, which results in more successful fusions than screws.

When we went back to the pain management doctor for the bone scan results, we learned that everything looked great. The screws were not wearing down the bone. The doctor said, "Doing the discogram would allow me to buy my wife a very nice Christmas gift, but I'm not going to do it. You don't need it."

He also told us that he saw no reason at all for my sacroiliac fusion in the first place, discounting my testimony of having moved from 13 years of disabling pain to three years of pain-free living after my double SI fusion. He was obviously of the camp that believed the SI joint cannot sublux. (He was the same doctor who had told me years ago to get up in the morning, make my bed, and not get back in it.)

At one point, he and my husband got into it. Honestly, I got a tinge of pleasure listening to my man defend me so passionately! I was struggling with depression and in no condition to handle this doctor's insensitive verbiage. Lying face down on the white paper padded table, I asked God to help me contain my emotions because my insides were boiling. I felt like I was seconds away from lashing out in anger and frustration or giving in to a gut-wrenching cry.

I can count seventy-two different health care providers that I have seen for my back pain. By far, most of them have tried to help me or have humbly admitted that they just don't understand and cannot help me. I've been desperate for doctors to understand just how awful my situation is.

There have been a few who, because they didn't understand, believed that I was making this up. I was told, "This (subluxation) cannot happen," and "You are doing this for attention," and "You just need to go to the YMCA and swim." And, really, why should they believe me when nothing wrong shows up on any of my tests? As if the pain, fear, and disappointment weren't enough, my character was in question. That ate away at me subtly because there was nothing that I could say or do to convince anyone with letters behind their name that I was authentically suffering and genuinely desperate.

I brought this frustration to God for the umpteenth time, when He whispered to my mind in empathy: "Yes, it stinks when people don't believe you, especially when your character proves truthful." Whoa! The very thing that exasperated me to no end, I had been doing with God. What grounds have I ever had to doubt the all-faithful One who made the whole universe and holds it all together?

He has proven to be ever true to His Word and to all of humankind since the dawn of His creation! Doubting what He has said in the Bible is to doubt His character. There I was, irked with my fellow man for judging my character when I was profoundly guilty of judging God's character, doubting His ability to provide, protect, or enable me. *Oh, what a foolish creature I am! God, please forgive me, forgive us!*

I thought the time spent in this doctor's office validated a few minutes of self-pity. But after my thinking cleared, I knew that this man's attitude inflicted a dose of emotional pain only because I had allowed it. The greatest waste of time and money wasn't on the bone scan, but on the emotional energy I had spent allowing what this man said to us to affect me for years to come.

I contacted Mrs. Sims and explained my situation with the discogram, so she arranged for me to have the discogram done by a willing pain management doctor in Gainesville, Georgia. Coordinating with three different offices in Georgia, my family doctor here, and the insurance company was challenging.

Getting to Georgia was no easy task either. Driving and flying were equally hard on me physically. While traveling by air is faster, I couldn't stand for more than a few minutes or sit for more than 15-20 minutes without getting into trouble. Once, when I got off an airplane, I crumbled to the ground in pain just a few steps into the airport. Embarrassing! Coping with my pain is not a matter of mind over will. Often it dictated my actions or lack of them, no matter how embarrassing. Being juggled and jarred about in a car also takes a big toll on me. Bumps are the absolute worst.

We decided to travel by car. My ingenious husband contoured a piece of plywood to fit in the backseat of our Toyota Corolla so I could lie down on a hard, flat surface. He put a piece of memory foam on top of the plywood that made my ride as comfortable as possible. It's a good thing that I'm only 5'3". If I were any taller, that arrangement wouldn't have worked.

Clad with the back-brace, TENS unit, ice packs, and medications, we left for Georgia on a Wednesday. The discogram test was scheduled for Friday and appointments with Mrs. Sims and Dr. Weiss on Monday, with a tentative surgery date the next day, December 18th.

Friends of ours from Papua New Guinea learned of our trip to Georgia through Facebook. They were house-sitting at a place 20 miles from Gainesville during their home assignment. Even though it was Christmas time, the Diepenbrocks kindly invited us to stay with them. We had a spacious bed and bath above the garage. They were a huge blessing to us, welcoming us, not just into their home, but into their lives.

During that time, I wrote this letter to a friend explaining more of what I was going through.

December 2012

Dear Sharon,

Thanks for walking through all this with me. What a journey it's been. Yesterday, when we were at the hospital for the pre-admission testing, my pain took over. We did all that we could to rein in the pain, but as we drove to Vicki's office from the hospital my pain was out of control.

By the time we arrived, I was unraveled and doing the Lamaze breathing to help cope with the pain. Although it's so embarrassing to have this happen in public, I think it was good for Vicki to see how fast things escalate. Immediately, she had someone hook me up with electrotherapy, which quickly calmed the spasm. (I need to find out how I can buy one of those ramped-up machines; it makes my little TENS unit seem like a toy.)

Mrs. Sims doesn't understand what's driving my pain, but she assured me that she believes me and has no plans of dropping me. I'm thankful for that! Today, she is going to ask Dr. Weiss to order me a nerve block at L5. After that injection, I am supposed to do things that I know will irritate my condition. (Should I ask to vacuum their office? That would send me over the edge!) If I still experience my typical pain, then it's on to the discogram. If those two tests rule out the disc, they will concede to re-fuse the right sacroiliac joint. I don't know if they can get me in for both of those tests this week.

Dr. Weiss could do the surgery on the 18th, but we just learned that Mrs. Sims is not available that day. Alignment is so crucial to the success of this surgery that we won't have this done without her. If they agree to do the surgery, it won't happen until sometime in the new year. Oh well. How can I complain? There are so many in this wide world that have no access to medical help. Regardless of what is causing the pain, Mrs. Sims doesn't see me living like this forever. I certainly hope not. Pain is so evil!

I've had a lot of pain these days. Thanks for keeping me in prayer, I sure need it. We know God doesn't turn a deaf ear to His children. Time and again, we've asked God to lead. I believe that He is; I just need to be patient as His plan unfolds.

Kerri

    The selective nerve root block did nothing to help my pain. One final test remained to rule out that the pain coming from the disc: the discogram. It was scheduled in Georgia for the 28th of January.

    The delay meant paying another year's insurance deductible and a third trip to Georgia. However, my heart was now at peace, which was priceless! Dr. Weiss and Mrs. Sims were on board to do the re-fusion on the 31st of January if the discogram failed to reproduce my pain. What a huge relief! I just didn't know what I was going to do if they weren't willing to do the re-fusion. I tried hard not to let my mind go there.

    The previous 750-mile trip home from Georgia in our car did not go well at all. But it was surprising to see how God supplied for this final trip to and from Georgia. Our friends, Rex and Laurie, offered us the use of their truck, which fit a twin-sized mattress behind the driver's seat. It was a very comfortable ride indeed. We received another incredible gift: our friends gave us their credit card and told us to charge our whole trip on it. Who does this sort of thing? Why us? What a gift!

    When our friends in Georgia heard that my surgery was postponed, right away they invited us to stay in their guestroom again! God was using these friends and many others who were praying to shower His love over us.

    As I expected, the discogram failed to reproduce my pain. Dr. Weiss and Vicki were both skeptical of this surgery helping me. The day before the surgery, Dr. Weiss told me that he thought there was less than a 10% chance that this would help. He and Mrs. Sims didn't believe that fusion would make a difference because the screws were in place.

    I still had very high hopes. Mrs. Sims told me that she was praying for me on her way to the hospital and during the surgery. Hundreds of people from all over were praying for all of us in the operating room that day.

Those three little I-fuse implants made a world of difference! Though this surgery defied reason, the third day after surgery I was free of pain medication, and I could sit erect in a regular chair, totally relaxed and with no back spasm. Imagine if the only thing that ever needed aligned again was my attitude!

One week after my surgery, I met with Dr. Weiss and Mrs. Sims. They were both shocked at how well I was doing. Vicki said she still had no explanation for why I was in so much pain previously or how it was that I was feeling such relief so quickly. Vicki said, "It must have been all the prayer!"

When I told her that my flare-ups were ten times worse than this recovery, she looked dumbfounded. Dr. Weiss said that I was supposed to be in a lot of pain after this surgery, but I wasn't! Both were surprised that I wasn't on any medication. Upon leaving the hospital, I took just one of the sixty narcotic pills they gave me for the drive from the hospital back to the house. Other than that, I didn't take anything for pain, not even Tylenol. (However, I would take one more for the flight back to Pennsylvania.)

Vicky encouraged me to avoid bending and twisting because of the fusion; the torque from those moments would not be distributed normally. With no movement in the SI joints, it would put unnatural stress on the joint between the last vertebrae and the sacrum. Also, with spondylolisthesis and degenerative discs, I needed to be careful not to create a situation that would require more surgery. I would need to be wise and develop good movement habits. I was so used to protecting that area that I just didn't bend.

While I was still in the hospital, our son, Jonathan, called me to ask if we had decided how we were getting home. His best friend, Alex, had offered to fly us back home; he had access to a plane. Since it was January, we would be dealing with ice and snow driving home. I told him we had not yet decided. An anonymous individual offered to pay for our fuel. God's provisions were piling up! I just didn't know if we should take advantage of all that or not. I knew we could make it home comfortably in the truck with the mattress. The problem would be getting in and out of the truck for bathroom breaks — the ice, snow, and crutches made for a greater fall risk. In my condition, falling while the I-fuse plugs were yet setting would be devastating, but I didn't know that at the time.

My son finally convinced me, saying, "Mom, if someone wants to do something nice for you, even if it's not an absolute necessity, I think you should let them have the joy of blessing you." So that's what we did.

Our friend, Rex, had a friend, BJ. And BJ knew Bill Elliot, NASCAR's 1988 Winston Cup Champion. Bill and his brother, Ernie, owned the field with an airstrip right across the road from the house where we were staying in Georgia. Not only did the Elliots permit Alex to land on their airstrip, but I found out years later that the Elliots also paid for the plane's fuel! And I never even met these generous people. Rex and BJ flew down to Georgia with Alex so they could drive the truck back to Pennsylvania, allowing Tim to fly back with me. Laurie had fixed a comfy bed for me on the plane and offered us yummy snacks on our flight back home. As the warm sun beamed in on my face on that flight home, I felt enveloped in such incredible love, peace, and provision that my heart was bursting with praise to God. I was basking in His love and the care of so many people. I was relieved of my pain and incredibly happy. Non-weight bearing for six weeks, some physical therapy, and I'd be good to go. Or so I thought.

A Closer Look at the ONE in the KNOW

I may have stumped the specialists, but never God. There's never been a second when God was unaware of the needs of my family and me. Many things can take us by surprise, holding the potential to rock us to the core. But not the omniscient God. He gets the whole scoop.

Though He welcomes my every word, I never need to explain myself to Him. Everything I've been through and will yet go through is known to God as well as my every thought, attitude, unfulfilled desire, action, and reaction. What's precious to me is that, despite knowing everything about me, God loves me completely! He welcomes all my unanswered questions and deep frustrations.

These are the questions that are always before me: Is it enough to know that God knows and cares? Can I be okay with not knowing the answers and find rest because God does?

Knowing all the answers is not my privilege or right but trusting Him is. Besides, having the answers doesn't necessarily change anything. Understanding all about a situation doesn't enable me to redeem it. I find that my fears of the unknown diminish as my relationship with the One who knows all grows.

CHAPTER 8

An Untamable Life of Its Own
2013-2015

I felt great! Swimming and floor exercises were going very well. I was getting stronger and stronger. With my new-found freedom, I could really play with our grandkids. I was able to join my coworkers, cooking and visiting with the guests on campus. Occasionally, I would even clean the guestrooms, carefully though, with smart body mechanics. Increasingly, I could get away with doing more and more because nothing hurt. Tim was even getting confident in my abilities and stopped cautioning me — until he saw me carrying one of our grandkids.

During those months of great health, our sixth grandchild was born. In the summer of 2013, we traveled to upstate New York to care for our grandsons Gabriel and Tyler, as Jessica gave birth to her third handsome son, Elijah.

I was sure that all those back problems were behind me. I'd been pain free for eighteen months!

Tim left in April of 2014 for Papua New Guinea to help install a second hydroelectric system for a hospital in Kudjip. They finished up a week early, and he made it home in time for Julie's delivery of our lovely little Abigail.

At this point, we were blessed with seven precious grandkids under the age of seven. I'm a nurturer at heart, and young children are my forte. I thoroughly loved snuggling, teaching, feeding, encouraging, and playing with each of them.

In mid-July, I drove up to Jessica's in New York to help watch the boys while she set up and ran a weekend yard sale. She was six months pregnant with their fourth child. During this visit, I tripped over a guitar case while I was carrying Elijah, who had just turned one. Suspending his weight in an extended position, I was able to keep him from hitting his head on the wood at the back of the couch. And somehow, I managed not to fall down. I didn't think I had the strength or balance to have done that. He was a heavy baby!

I thought it strange that I didn't suffer any consequences the next morning. But back home four mornings later, I woke up stiff, but I headed to the dining hall as it was my day to cook for the guests on campus. In the evening, I trudged up the small but steep hill behind our house for the campfire meeting. After that jaunt, I began having pain that didn't let up, even after I lay down on a cabin porch. In fact, the pain steadily increased. Back home, I took pain medicine, lay on an icepack, and went to bed.

I woke up feeling fine, so I headed to the office to put together some visitors' packages. Soon after I began working, I felt some tension in my lower back. I adjusted everything so that I could sit down to do my work, confident that that would take the stress off my back. Just a few minutes later, I started feeling nauseous. *Hmm. Am I getting sick? Oh, I hope not! If I am, I shouldn't be around all these people.* Those were my immediate thoughts. How I wish it had been a stomach flu. I would have rather had a week of that than many weeks of severe, incapacitating pain.

This flare-up began as Tim was approaching the end of a month-long stay in Kenya, helping to install another hydroelectric generator system for a hospital. We would touch base usually at least once a day. We didn't FaceTime because my iPod had recently gone through the wash and was drying out in a bag of rice. If we had, I wouldn't have been able to hide my pain from him. He had recently gotten sick over there, and I didn't want him to spend his energy worrying about me. I was planning to tell him about my condition when he was well into his journey home. But when I answered one of his texts, when he knew I would have otherwise been at church, I was found out.

After my last surgery I had mentioned to Vicki that my flare-ups were ten times worse than surgery; actually, some are closer to 50 times worse. And when my orthopedic prescribed 60 oxycodone pills after my SI fusion, I used two, but only because Tim wanted me to have something for pain in my system for traveling, as the bumps really affect me, even when lying down. During this flare-up, I used all of those remaining pills plus a few more prescriptions of narcotics, in addition to muscle relaxants, anti-inflammatory and steroid medications, plus trigger point injections. Pain from surgery usually lasts a day or two, but I never know how long the severe pain of a flare-up will last. This tremendous one lasted eight weeks. Tim returned home during the second week of the flare-up. What in the world had gone wrong now?

I was not sleeping. My doctor increased my antidepressant dosage and started me on a new medication that was supposed to help with nerve pain and with sleep. Still, I was only able to get two or three hours of sleep. Unfortunately, the latest trip to the doctor's office had thrown me into extremely severe pain.

These weeks resurrected another problem that I had dealt with before when I was in extreme pain, but never to this magnitude. Around the clock, day after day, I struggled to urinate. I overheard Tim tell the urologist that, on average, it was taking me twenty minutes to release any urine. Sometimes we were close to leaving for the emergency room just to be catharized. This extremely frustrating problem meant that I was sitting up much longer than my back wanted which made relaxing that much harder.

Two weeks later, I was worse. Tim got a bedside toilet for me because I'd been crawling to and from the bathroom. Twice that week I crawled down the stairs and out to the car, once for my MRI and once to go to the doctor. We requested a gurney to transport me from our vehicle to the MRI room, but they wouldn't allow it. I would have rather crawled the distance than to have sat in that wheelchair; every bump was excruciating. If all this wasn't bad enough, that day turned out to be the worst day ever of dealing with my menopausal issues. Sometimes when it rains, it just pours. After the MRI, they pushed me to our car on a gurney.

That week I sent a text to Tyler, a friend of ours who was suffering from Lyme disease. I explained how extremely weak and needy I was and asked him to pray for me. His response was one of the wisest things anyone has ever told me: "We're all just as desperately needy as you are; it's just that you're keenly aware of it right now." He was right! Those timely words of wisdom were so comforting, as I realized I was not alone in my desperately needy condition. None of us are in control; we are completely dependent beings! We can't make our hearts beat or our lungs breathe. We can plant seeds in the dirt, but we're powerless to make anything grow. We can dig wells, but we're unable to make water appear. We simply cannot sustain ourselves. We are all equally and utterly needy for God's mercy; without it, we would all be consumed.

Neediness and adversity are tools that God has used to show me my insufficiency and sinfulness. They have paved a path for greater dependence on Him. We raise our children to become independent and rightfully so. But God raises His children to become wholly dependent on Him because that is what's best for us. Shouldn't I be thankful that God refuses my requests that feed my inclination to live independent of Him? In light of that, could I eventually welcome these trials? Do I trust God enough to ask for whatever difficulty He sees best to keep me relying on Him?

I'm bent to live for the "here and now," while God is eternally minded. He has promised an everlasting reward for my faithfulness to Him in this life. To spare me the consequences of suffering through life apart from Him, I experience trials that keep me depending on His mercy and grace. In the chorus of Laura Story's song "Blessings," she suggests, in the form of a question, that perhaps the trials of our lives are God's mercies in disguise.[12] God's economy *is* vastly different from mine. I'd bet my bottom dollar that He values faith and godly character way more than temporary comfort and limited happiness. God is zealous to save me from sin, self-rule, and independence from Him because He knows what's best for me in the long run.

The day after the MRI, I asked my doctor for a Medrol Dosepak steroid. Under my breath, I said that I wish I could have some Lidocaine injections. He was happy to oblige. Those shots brought significant relief beyond the intended three to four hours. They seemed to "shock" my system, allowing it to calm down. I was now able to stand, rather than crawl. In hope to calm my nerve pain, the doctor added Gabapentin to my medication regiment, but I immediately developed mouth sores.

As the muscle spasms waned, I started back on the treadmill, slowly walking one minute every hour or two depending on whether I was too worn out from sitting too long on the toilet.

The first week in September, I went back to Shari for physical therapy in the pool. Looking back through our notes from that appointment, we saw that Shari had mentioned "an *autonomic nervous system dysfunction*" and *"central sensitization"* as factors in my condition. Yet it did not register in our minds as something to research.

Because the drive to and from therapy was too hard on me, we decided to go up the road to our friend's swimming pool. I absolutely loved the anti-gravity effect of the water, allowing me to move around. The beauty of nature surrounding me up on that mountain was a sanctuary, a hiatus from my dreary bedroom.

These two journal entries taken from two consecutive days of this back flare-up show how quickly things can develop with very little change in stimuli.

***Day 42:** Tim was nervous about me overdoing it in the pool, so he encouraged me to move very little and float often. I listened. It felt so good to be in the water; the pressure in my low back was gone due to the buoyancy, I guess. I didn't want to get out. I realized that I could enjoy weightlessness at home when the bathtub is full of water — good thing I'm short. I'm so happy to be at the point where I can get to this pool and get my own drinks. Pretzels and almonds are my standby when Tim's not around to fix me something. I recently stood long enough to slice a homegrown tomato. Was it ever good! Progress is so slow, but I am pulling out of this mess.*

***Day 43:** I'm incredibly frustrated! I got in the pool again today, but I didn't just float. I focused on keeping my knees together and took tiny baby steps. But I kicked my legs just a little bit, only from the knees down. I kept my knees together so my hips and pelvis wouldn't move. But before my half hour in the water was up, I was hurting. "Setbacks always happen, Kerri," Tim reminded me. But they're so disheartening. I was back on ice, medication, and the TENS unit. How was I to know that something so drastic could come from such tiny movement in the water?*

I was confined to bed, rotating ice packs, and taking narcotics for a week before the back spasm began to let up. I bemoaned feeling like I was back at square one after wading through such a lengthy rehab. After a couple of decades, you would think that we would've figured out how to move from flare-up to function successfully. Obviously, we hadn't. Somehow, this seemed like a different ball game, with no rules to play by. How in the world did this whole mess start anyway? Tripping over a guitar case. That's just crazy!

Patience. Patience. Patience. During this flare-up in particular, I was trying to learn the discipline of not looking ahead or behind, but just focusing on right now. God gives me grace for my need right when I need it; I won't find it for the future.

Autumn arrived, so Tim started taking me to the pool at the YMCA. During the next three weeks, I finally made steady progress swimming in the water. I had improved so much that I asked Tim to take me to our local farmer's market. There is nothing like a trip to the farmer's market in the fall to boost my spirits. It was only a five-minute drive to the market, and we were there and back in no more than fifteen minutes. I carried nothing. But I sat up in the car just for the ride home, and it was my undoing. I spent the rest of the day and the next weeping. We both thought I was ready for the little outing. *Hadn't I built up to it? Couldn't I read my body well enough? How would I ever know when it was safe to add activity outside of water?*

Tim was rather perceptive on when it was time for me to take a narcotic, and he would document each one I took. Over the years, I'd been tempted at times to take one when I just wasn't feeling well but didn't truly need it. But I never did. I knew that was a dangerous door to open, and once it cracked just a bit, it would make it that much easier to open it a bit further the next time. I was determined to not let anything like that further complicate my life.

Ten days after the farmer's market fiasco, we decided to go to the YMCA for some pool therapy. Five minutes into the drive, I had to ask Tim to turn around and take me back home. I couldn't tolerate the road, even lying down on the back seat. Back home, Tim brought me my TENS unit. For some reason during that time, we just hadn't thought of using it until then. I don't know how it was, that I could fight so many battles with pain and *still* not have remembered all of my weapons of defense! The next day, with the TENS unit on, I managed the jaunt to my doctor for more Lidocaine injections. Using the TENS unit allowed me to cut back on my narcotic intake.

I had now been on ice packs around the clock for eight weeks. I had no appetite but had to eat a little bit anyway. From previous flare-ups, I'd learned that digestion is greatly affected when you don't move around or sit up. So tiny portions worked best. This time, I learned something else: don't take new medicine along with your old medicine; it could be a bad combination! The bubbling burned my esophagus so that I could only comfortably eat things that were cold and smooth for the next six weeks. It was the perfect excuse for eating ice cream!

The second week in October, I was spasm free. For the next three weeks, I was able to walk on the treadmill three times a day and swim once a week. Moving outside of water was much harder, so all my "up time" (when I was not in bed) I used for exercise. Plus, I could sit up when I ate, but too long in that position, and the heavy, painful pressure kicked in.

In the middle of the calamity, God parted the clouds to give us our fourth granddaughter, Raven, a bundle of heaven-sent sunshine! Jessica and her family came to visit us just as soon as she was able to travel. Meeting this sweet baby was balm for my soul. Just like me, Raven would grow up with three older brothers. Trying to describe my love for these grandkids is like trying to explain color to the blind. I just can't.

On November 9th, I had my first social outing since mid-July; I went to church. In general, social settings make me apprehensive and Tim stressed. It's challenging to be with people, while trying to avoid them in certain situations, yet not be rude. When I'm in a social setting, I have to get myself comfortably seated quickly. People don't know or remember that standing for any length of time ramps up my pain. I have to keep walking and make no eye contact, or if someone does engage me in conversation, I need to invite them to walk with me.

In the early years of my back issues, I could engage with people and push the pain into the background. Now the stakes were much higher. The pain would escalate so quickly. I wouldn't have long to respond before I was in big trouble. I needed to shut down conversations at the first inkling of trouble, which was hard for me to do. My family was vigilant to come rescue me in public settings if they thought that I'd been standing too long. They knew from experience that if I stood just a couple minutes too long once I was already maxed out, it would add insult to injury, possibly putting me down for days or weeks.

There always has to be a first time to jump back into things after a flare-up. I thought my outing to church that day went pretty well, but when I got out of bed the next morning, the pain hit. Just moving around a little bit revealed that I was going straight downhill. The following day was worse, although we were doing everything that we knew to do to arrest the pain. I was on a slippery slope. I was trying hard to find "traction" before the pain picked up any more momentum. It seemed like this pain had an untamable life of its own.

After another week in bed using ice packs, the TENS unit, narcotics, and more Lidocaine injections, my pain was still not under control. Hoping I had not outworn my welcome, we went back to the doctor for more Lidocaine injections. Sadly, they only helped for three hours this time. Then I was out of my mind with the pain. Somehow, I made it through that night. At several points, I wanted to go to the ER, but I had a dreadful fear of the drive to get there. I held out until morning when Tim phoned the doctor's office. This time, I was given a script for pain patches, Lyrica, and another round of steroids. Thankfully the doctor didn't require me to come in.

The next day, my doctor's office was able to set up two appointments for me. Because of cancellations due to a snowstorm, I was able to be seen by a new pain management doctor in town and the orthopedic doctor. The new arsenal of drugs from the day before helped rein in the pain enough for us to drive to those appointments.

The pain management doctor said there was nothing more she could do for me other than what my family physician had already done. When the orthopedic reviewed my MRIs and X-rays, he saw very little change since my last set of imaging. There was movement in a few of the lower vertebrae, but he didn't think it was excessive. However, the thing that grabbed his attention was my reflexes. On a scale of one to four, reflexes should be a two; mine was at four, meaning hyper-reflexive. He thought this "hyperreflexia" could be an indicator of something happening in the middle of my back, so he ordered a thoracic MRI and referred me to a neurosurgeon.

Since the late '90s, whenever my body was stressed, I would start jerking uncontrollably. These jerks, known as myoclonic jerks, make different groups of muscles all over the body jerk at various intervals. Tim said I would jerk and twitch in my sleep too. Now we wondered if these jerks and hyperreflexia were somehow related to the autonomic nervous system issue that my physical therapist had suspected.

The neurosurgeon had no explanation for my hyperreflexia, urination problems, or myoclonic jerks. He said that sometimes the thyroid could present these kinds of symptoms, so he referred me to a medical neurologist.

This doctor ordered a cervical MRI, which showed "multi-leveled disc disease with some spinal cord involvement." But the only significant, consistent neck pain I had ever had was part of the chain reaction when my SI joint was misaligned. This neurologist found a positive Hoffman's reflex, which perhaps pointed to spinal compression or a nerve condition. We were getting clues, but no diagnosis.

This season of relentless pain, with no reason for the pain, led to a torrent of frustration. I struggled against an endless whirlpool of disappointment that threatened to pull me under. I was fighting against lies, fear, and confusion, while I was fighting for peace, contentment, and comfort.

Throughout these years, God repeatedly showed me the importance of speaking truth to myself; He wanted me to filter the thoughts coming into my mind. Left to my natural inclination, my thoughts would be manufactured by my feelings, my sinful desires, and my pagan culture. Unbridled thoughts contain lies, self-condemnation, pessimism, and despair. When I'm fearful and worried, I have to pull out my "truth sieve" to sift away the lies and savor the truth that remains.

I love what Corrie Ten Boom says: "Worry does not empty tomorrow of its sorrow. It empties today of its strength."[13] Worry borrows trouble that I do not own. God knows I've had enough trouble without borrowing more. When I realize that I'm worrying, I have to grab the reins of my mind; otherwise, I would trot over to the land of "what-ifs."

Author Paul Tripp says, "Worry finds a foothold in the lie that you're alone in your suffering. Meanwhile, the Lord names Himself Immanuel — God with us. Worry will tell you that you need to carry the burden on your shoulders; Immanuel says, 'I will carry it for you.'"[14]

In the new year, 2015, I was doing better. I could sit up in the car for short rides. Urinating was much easier, but still not easy. It seemed that we had exhausted the help available in our city, and I still had no answers.

Our son Jonathan had a friend who was an orthopedic surgeon. When this doctor heard about my quandary, he graciously offered his help, so I began corresponding with him in March. After he had reviewed my tests and found nothing unusual, he asked if anyone had ever suggested a spinal cord stimulator. I'd never heard of such a thing before. He said it might help block unnecessary pain signals. I was intrigued!

In April, our ninth grandchild was born. Jolie gave birth to Camryn, our blonde cutie-pie! Carter was now a big brother. In just eleven months, God had gifted us with three darling granddaughters. I remember the family get-togethers in our small apartment being quite loud in those days.

A few days after Camryn's birth, I had an appointment in the Philadelphia area to meet the pain specialist that Jonathan's doctor friend had recommended. A facet joint injection confirmed that the pain was not coming from the spinal joints. A month later, we traveled back to Philly to get hooked up with a trial spinal cord stimulator. An external battery pack was connected to internal leads along my spinal cord to see if it would help my pain. After that procedure, I enjoyed five wonderful pain-free days.

In mid-June, I had a consultation with Dr. Ashwini Sharan, a world-renowned expert in the field of neuromodulation, at Jefferson Memorial Hospital in Philadelphia. Surprisingly, he walked into the room and announced that he would not implant the spinal cord stimulator as he did not think it was the best option for me at that point. His advice was to see a kidney specialist first because he saw something suspicious on my MRI.

Dr. Sharan said he was not taking the spinal cord stimulator completely off the table. The kind of stimulator he used had paddles that required the removal of some vertebral bone in order to attach the leads, leaving you with a compromised vertebra. He said that he has had to remove implants from many patients like me because the device had only been useful for about five years. (He had no idea how absolutely wonderful five pain-free years sounded to me!) The doctor felt it would be more advantageous for us to continue digging for a diagnosis and suggested that we go to the Mayo Clinic. While we saw the wisdom in his counsel, it surely was disappointing. However, we had been asking God to lead us, so we took this as His answer.

I felt like somewhat of a tight-rope walker in the whole thing: keeping pain and stress levels down, taking as little pain medication as possible, but as much as necessary, being as active as possible without setting anything off. It seemed like I no sooner would get my balance when I'd fall off again. In July, I succumbed to yet another major flare-up. A few months later I wrote the following letter to a few close friends.

September 9, 2015

Dear Sharon and Lynette,

Ladies, I could sure use more prayer! These are tough circumstances: the pain, the confinement, and the difficulty urinating.

I have been pondering thankfulness and its connection to joy. I'm thankful for the opportunity to have joy and comfort regardless of these adverse circumstances. But it's been hard! Yet, ironically, these are precious times.

I'm so thankful that God has given me a strong husband who devotedly bears this burden with me! Few women can say that they have lovingly been served breakfast in bed every day for two months!

Tim has also been softly singing songs with me in the bathroom too. This has been helping me relax enough to pee. Occupying my mind with positive thoughts is helping me counter the discouragement, which makes me more tense.

I flip my thankful switch on and off all day long! I wake up, thankful that I can get out of bed, then the pain hits, and I'm not thankful I have a bed to go back to.

I'm thankful that I live in a country where I can go to a qualified doctor, and then I grumble about the potholes on the way to the office.

I'm grateful to have Tim in the room with me as I nervously wait for the doc to come, yet I grumble in my heart about putting on another thin, tied-in-the-back gown.

I praise God that I don't have cancer, then I groan: Why can't anybody on the face of this earth see what is causing my pain?

For all of us, the more difficult our circumstances, the more crucial it is to focus on gratitude. Being thankful is linked to my confidence in God's promises.

As His child, rejoicing in Him, being thankful to Him, and being anxious for nothing are imperatives, not suggestions. They are my means to peace and godliness. Like I said, I need prayer, because it's so hard.

Thanks for holding me up,

Kerri

We applied to John's Hopkins Hospital in Baltimore because the Mayo Clinic, where Dr. Sharan had suggested, was so far away. I couldn't fathom traveling to Baltimore either, but we had to do something; I needed more help. In the meantime, two different friends of ours told us about a neurologist an hour away. They thought he would be worth pursuing. Fortunately, this doctor traveled to a second office near our town twice a month.

While I am thankful for the privilege to have access to all sorts of doctors and specialists, as so many people in this world do not, I dreaded going to a new doctor. But there was no need for trepidation with this doctor. Dr. Askari's demeanor was refreshing! Kind and humble, he told us that God is the healer and that he is merely the conduit. We couldn't have agreed more. Because of miscommunications between the doctor's office, the hospital and me, it took seven weeks to schedule an MRI. Unbelievable!

While I waited, I wrote the following letter to a friend.

December 10, 2015

Dear Katie,

This year of tsunami-size back flare-ups pounded me mercilessly. I've been so overwhelmed, trying in vain to find a reason for my out-of-control back pain. Major frustration easily consumes me when I can't see an inch of progress.

It seems like we've done everything to try to find the reason for pain and deal with it. In the last fourteen months I've had several sets of X-rays, eight MRIs, two CT scans, a facet joint block, a temporary spinal stimulator implanted, an electroencephalogram, a nerve conduction study, an ultrasound, a CT scan of the kidney, a nuclear medicine bone scan, a spinal tap, many trips to the doctor for trigger point injections of Lidocaine, and physical therapy. I've joked with Tim, that if I had saved all my appointment cards over the last 30 years, I'd be able to wallpaper a room with them.

So far, we've learned that I have a cyst on my right kidney that is a non-issue, different issues in my back and neck (none that standout as severe pain generators), and various neurological symptoms that point to spinal cord dysfunction. There is a mid-sized lesion in my brain that typically would give migraines and loss of coordination; thankfully, I have neither.

But none of these tests explain my severe pain. My physical therapist thinks I am dealing with lumbar instability and some type of autonomic nervous system dysfunction. She said that my "fight or flight" mode just doesn't turn off. I agree!

I'm learning that I can't rely on my own pain signals to guide me. Once I begin to sense pain, the vortex is suddenly in motion, and inflammation has already ensued. These last two major flare-ups spun out of control for months on end before we could get the pain managed for any level of function. In the thick of those severe flare-ups, brushing my teeth was too much movement. This level of severe on-going pain just sucks the life out of you.

Katie, thanks for listening, caring, and praying. I certainly need it!

Kerri

Back in 1996, a deep-seated peace had anchored me while a raging tempest of pain had enveloped my body during my three weeks of hospitalization in Caracas. Then six months later, after going through yet another horrendous bout of weeks-on-end, out-of-control pain, I had not even an inkling of peace. Never before had I been so utterly desperate on every level: physically, emotionally, spiritually, and mentally (a severe depression was right around the corner). In maddening frustration, I slammed my fist on the kitchen table and declared, "The peace is mine!" I couldn't do anything more physical than that to express my anger. I thought that "the peace that surpasses all understanding" (Philippians 4:7) was supposed to guard my heart and mind. I was losing mine. Confusion ruled. Since peace is a fruit of the Spirit of God who lives within me, wasn't I supposed to have peace at all times? Were there circumstances that would negate my peace? Was mental illness an exemption from that peace — only available when my mind wasn't sick? Maintaining peace was very important to me because I was fighting the battle of my life.

I struggled with a Bible verse from Isaiah 26:3: "You will keep in perfect peace those whose minds are steadfast, because they trust in you."

Jesus, the Prince of Peace, paid a very high price for my peace, and I wanted to know why I didn't have it. With all my heart, I trusted in Jesus, at least the best I knew how. Why wasn't He keeping me in "shalom, shalom" (perfect peace) as the Hebrew text said? God keeps His promises. So why wasn't I experiencing that promised peace that I'd experienced in my previous major crisis?

The meaning of the word "peace" in Hebrew and Greek texts has a richer and deeper meaning than just the absence of strife and antagonism. It conveys wholeness, completeness, and fulfillment in things, activities and in relationships between people and nations, as well as between God and man.

This "perfect peace" is about my position before God. The verb form of the Hebrew word *peace* means to join or bind together, to restore what was broken or separated. Before I became a child of God, I was at war with Him. Then when I trusted in the sacrificial death of Jesus on my behalf, my broken relationship with God was restored. He issued a declaration of peace toward me. No matter what danger seems to threaten, forevermore I have perfect peace with God. Just as I can be loved by God, yet not feel His love, I can have peace in my relationship with Him without sensing His peace. Now when I look at that verse in Isaiah, I realize that this peace is not about a fleeting feeling, it's so much more!

What I focus on affects my emotions, attitude, mind, and even my health to some degree. The tranquility of my mind is "perfect" or "imperfect" to the degree that my "mind is stayed on" God rather than on myself or my problems.

Once a group of friends fought a furious squall, and they feared for their lives. Waves were crashing over their boat, filling it with water faster than they could empty it. They were in an impossible situation in which they could not save themselves. They woke Jesus from a sound sleep and asked Him if he even cared about what they were facing. Jesus merely spoke to the sea, and the storm stopped immediately! I imagine a sense of peace washed over them in an instant. Realize that these disciples (for that is who this group of friends were) of Jesus were just as safe before He spoke to the sea as they were afterward. The storm stirred up fearful emotions and robbed them of their sense of peace. But their proximity to Jesus in that boat made them safe even though they did not have a sense of peace or safety.

My American concept of the word "peace" is a feeling of inner calm that we have when our circumstances are favorable. This, however, is not the peace of God. If peace is a result of great circumstances, then why, when our nation has some of the best circumstances on the planet, do we lack peace? Easy circumstances may have little to do with personal peace.

The peace of God is having our broken relationship with Him restored; only then is there wholeness and harmony with our Creator God. I've been wholly at peace this whole time!

I am constantly faced with a choice: frustrate myself by focusing on why God doesn't choose to heal me or focus on all He wants to teach me in this journey. God has loftier goals for me than my comfort and happiness. He seems more passionate about working miracles in my character than in my body. God keeps reminding me that healing is not supposed to be my primary goal in life. God is teaching me to trust Him with my pain, disappointments, and unanswered questions. He is showing me that His grace can hold me no matter the size of the waves.

A Closer Look at MERCY and GRACE

Mercy. Do you find yourself complaining because you don't get what you feel you deserve? I do. Yet, looking at the big picture, I'll be eternally grateful that I didn't get what I deserved: eternal separation from God and all His goodness. Because of God's mercy, He delivers me from the just judgment I deserved and gives me forgiveness! Everything that is above eternal condemnation is God's mercy!

Grace is God's undeserved and unmerited favor. Because God is gracious, He gives me physical gifts of grace: family, friends, health, food, and fun. But more importantly, He gives me eternal gifts of grace like forgiveness, relationship, and eternal life. Even now God's grace is at work with me, helping me to grow in trusting Him and to act more like Him. I need His customized grace to match the shade of each trial. In these trials, God is wanting me to experience His grace more than healing in order to make known in yet another life the power of His sustaining grace.

Romans 8:32 says: "He who did not spare His own Son, but gave Him up for us all how will He not also, along with Him, graciously give us all things?"

God's amazing grace saved a wretch like me! And because of that, He will graciously give me every spiritual blessing that He knows I need, including peace.

CHAPTER 9

Misery Loves Company

PERHAPS ABOUT 1440 BC

Why is there evil, pain, and suffering? What is the meaning of life? Why do we exist? People from every ethnic group on the planet struggle to answer those questions. And most of us have our own personal questions that we wrestle with.

Recovering from my deep depression in 1997, I struggled with some unanswered, lingering questions. I was so plagued by these questions that it seemed as though I couldn't move forward in life until I had answers. The more intensely I suffered, the more crucial the answers became. Sometimes I asked questions out of humility and a desire to understand, but other times out of arrogance and anger.

Once I heard someone say, "It's not about knowing all the answers, but about knowing God." That helped me start thinking about changing my perspective on questions.

It would have been futile for Tim and me to explain to Julie, when she was a newborn, why we allowed a phlebotomist to stick her with so many needles when she was in the intensive care unit. But all that poking wasn't in vain. It showed the doctors that she needed a blood transfusion. In a similar way, maybe it would've been futile for God to have explained things to me. Most likely, I wouldn't have been able to comprehend His answers.

Some of my big questions centered around my mental illness and my faith in God. My mental illness seemed to add a dimension to my suffering that profoundly affected my spiritual well-being. Why couldn't I perceive God's love or His peace? Was there a glitch in my thinking processes affecting the perception of my beliefs or were my beliefs wrong? Where was I not appropriating the truths of God's Word?

Our Creator knows all the answers, and He isn't bothered, threatened, or manipulated by any of our questions. While God welcomes them, He's not obligated to answer them. Since those days of consuming queries, I've discovered that I'm usually not asking the better questions.

Pastor David B. Curtis of Berean Bible Church in Virginia Beach, Virginia said, "The real difficult question is not, 'How could God allow us to suffer?' but 'How could He allow us, who rebel against His authority every day, to ever experience pleasure?' The mystery is why God would allow pleasure in the lives of those who hate Him and do not obey His commands."[15]

I came to realize that the better questions I could ask would be: Why was I born in a country with optimal health care? Does God owe me good health? Is He indebted to me or I to Him? What do I have of real value that has not come at the price of suffering? If the only thing I deserve is God's wrath, why do I receive mercy and grace? Why do I think I need to be spared of suffering if Jesus was not?

Many of my questions about suffering were answered through studying the compelling story of the ancient patriarch Job. During the worst year of my life, I limited my Bible reading exclusively to the books of Job and Jeremiah, the weeping prophet. Misery loves company!

In Job, I found a companion who struggled to reconcile his wretched, dire circumstances with his faithful, loving Creator. Satan believed that Job only loved and served God because He had greatly blessed him with a big, beautiful family, remarkable wealth, prestige, honor, and protection. Unknown to Job, Satan challenged God: "Stretch out Your hand and strike all that Job has, and he will surely curse You to Your face."[16]

Satan received permission to inflict evil on what belonged to Job, but not on Job himself. In one sad and sorry day, Job lost every bit of his immense wealth and all ten of his beloved children. "At this,

Job got up, tore his robe, and shaved his head. Then he fell to the ground in worship and said: 'Naked I came from my mother's womb, and naked I will depart. The Lord gave, and the Lord has taken away; may the name of the Lord be praised.' In all of this, Job did not sin by charging God with wrongdoing."[17] What a remarkable example of integrity!

Satan challenged God a second time: "Stretch out your hand and strike his flesh and bones, and he will surely curse you to your face."[18] God then released Job into Satan's hands, but he was not allowed to take his life.

Satan afflicted this poor man's entire body with boils. The original Hebrew may indicate they were so close together and thick, that it was as if there were one humongous maggot-infested boil covering his entire body.

In his anguish Job said, "I have sewed sackcloth over my skin and buried my brow in the dust."[19] Perhaps his oozing boils and ulcers grew layers of skin and attached it to his pus-soaked sackcloth, as he sat in an ash heap. His condition is too painful to imagine.

Job loathed the silence of God, as did I. He felt that God had dealt with him unfairly; I could relate. Job felt abandoned and needed assurance that God loved him; I did, too! We both had more questions than answers. I empathized with Job's struggle to trust God in the dark.

When I sat at the crossroads, wondering whether to continue trusting God when it seemed that He was against me, Job's example of integrity encouraged me to stay in there with God.

Job wanted to speak to the Almighty in order to argue his case. "Only grant me these two things, God, and then I will not hide from you: Withdraw your hand far from me, and stop frightening me with your terrors. Then summon me, and I will answer, or let me speak, and you reply to me."[20]

God allowed Job a hearing, but it didn't go as he had planned. He did not get answers to his questions. Instead, God asked Job seventy-seven rhetorical questions that had nothing to do with his pain and suffering. God's questions showed Job his ignorance and impotence. Job had been more confident in his own concept of fairness than in God's. Job's teaspoon-sized understanding of the situation didn't compare with God's limitless knowledge of all. The questions God asked transformed Job's perspective and ushered in an attitude of pure humility. God asks the better questions!

I believe that if Job had gotten all the answers to his questions, he would have continued serving God for all the wrong reasons. His motives for serving God would've been for the esteem and the fame that was coming his way.

Notice, it was Satan's idea to hurt Job. God is not the author of suffering, pain, evil, and injustice; He detests all of it! As darkness is the absence of light, so evil is the absence of good, the absence of God. Evil is not a created thing. But God allowed for the possibility of evil when He gave man the freedom to choose to obey and follow Him — or not.

Adam and Eve unleashed the forces of evil when they chose to believe Satan and throw off God's authority over them by eating that forbidden fruit. If God hadn't given mankind choice, then we would be nothing more than programmed robots.

Satan wanted to unmask Job as a fraud. He wanted to prove that God was not loved for simply who He was, but that He was a means to an end for Job. Satan studies humanity and knows that we tend to "love" with selfish motives. But God knew there would be those who would love Him freely and not for what they could get out of Him. (Initially, we all come to God because of our neediness.) God allowed the Devil's corrupt scheme only long enough to bring defeat to him and his wicked intentions. Satan didn't think that Job would hang in there with God. But he was wrong. In an odious, dark season of massive suffering, we observe that Job loved and served God even when it appeared that God was against him, disclosing his love for God as the real deal.

The only way I'll know that I'm honoring God for who He is rather than the benefits of His blessings is if I'm in a condition where I'm not getting anything out of serving God. Suffering without answers teaches me to love God and serve Him because He is worthy and not for any earthly perks.

Redeemed beyond Job's wildest imagination, God gave him ten more children, doubled his previous fortune, restored his good name, and honored Job by entering his story in the number one bestseller book of all times. Ironically, Satan's plan accomplished the opposite of what he purposed. For millennia, Job's example of integrity and devotion led the way for myriads of sufferers to follow in his footsteps. What Satan meant for Job's destruction, God used for so much good!

I am one of the millions of people who have benefited from Job's calamity. His story teaches me that my back pain is not a punishment because God is angry with me. My back pain is the result of being born into a sin-cursed world that He longs to redeem. This narrative shows me that I can openly and honestly express my raw grief and bitter sorrow to God. Job was not accused of sin for any of the raw emotions that he spewed. God knows this life is painful. He wants us to take our feelings to Him. Job freely laid out his pain and frustration before God, while still holding Him in honor for who He is.

The Bible says that we should, "Be angry and yet not sin."[21] Anger is a natural human emotion. In and of itself, anger is not bad. In fact, suppressing and burying anger can be detrimental.

At the end of the book, Job said to the Lord, "I know that you can do all things; no purpose of yours can be thwarted. You asked, 'Who is this that obscures my plans without knowledge?' Surely, I spoke of things I did not understand, things too wonderful for me to know."[22]

Job was not worthy to judge the wisdom of what God allowed — and neither am I. There is no ability within me to control the evil influences of Satan. I can't run this world. Nor could I ever take any form of evil and redeem it for good. Like Job, I too have "spoken of things I did not understand, things too wonderful for me to know." I cannot see the connection of my suffering to the world around me, but God can. Therefore, I should confidently say: "God, Your will be done." His actions are not arbitrary and uncalculated but full of good purpose, better than I can imagine!

The account of Job has helped me release my unanswered questions and appreciate the mystery by understanding that suffering can be a blessing in disguise. May it be enough for me to know that God has all the answers and that He doesn't disclose them for good reasons. It doesn't make my suffering less painful, but it does help me rest in God's love and trust in His sovereignty. I believe that as I co-operate with God, He won't waste my suffering. He loves me too much to waste it! God's love for us is too deep to give us lesser things.

The bedrock of my whole life is based on the fact that God loves me. However, during my deep depression, I wrestled to believe that fact, though I still believed that God loved everyone else in the whole world. Even though I was told, "Don't doubt in the night what God showed you in the day," I couldn't help but wonder, "How could I not?" Truly, I was questioning God's character. It was as if I brought God into the courtroom of my mind and put Him on trial.

I had some questions for God: "Have you really done everything You promised You would do for me? If You really love me, why have You allowed this degree of pain and suffering? If You are with me, why aren't You allowing me to sense Your presence?"

Beyond questions, I had nothing to say to God. My soul felt empty. But there were no other saviors, no one else to turn to. Rebelling wasn't the answer. It was hard enough to bear the dreadful suffering, but to feel unloved and rejected by God made it ten times worse. There is never more need for the assurance of God's love than in the crucible of suffering.

Now more than ever before, when gazing intently at the meaning of the crucifixion of Jesus Christ, I've found no better example of selfless love. Jesus, who is complete in God, does not need any of us or our love. With no selfish motives, He submitted to all that God the Father had asked of Him. Abandoned by God, Jesus endured crucifixion and hell (the wrath of God) for the greatest good of humanity.

God asked this of His most treasured Son to demonstrate His love for us. It may seem an evil thing for God the Father to ask His Son to endure such a death. This conflict dissolves when we understand that the Father, Son, and Holy Spirit are one being. God wanted the condemnation of the human race to be placed on Himself.

From the viewpoint of Jesus' disciples, His whole plan to set up the kingdom of God on earth crumbled before their eyes the day He was crucified. But three days later, when they saw the risen Christ, they began to understand the brilliance of the Master's plan of salvation for the whole world. All the pieces of the puzzle finally started to come together right before their eyes. Jesus' innocent suffering was not in vain; for through it, He redeems all who come to Him. Now, whenever I'm tempted to doubt God's love for me, I remember what Jesus suffered for me. It is all the proof I should ever need to convince me that God indeed loves me very much!

As for all of my questions, I know of no better place to look for answers for the meaning of pain and suffering than the Bible. The Bible doesn't give me a specific revelation about my personal suffering, but it gives me enough general answers for the framework of life to make sense. Its gives timeless wisdom, warnings, and instructions for the important aspects of life and helps me unmask the general *value of suffering*. *(See Appendix)* Value that will surpass my time on this earth.

A Closer Look at UNFAILING LOVE

"There is no pit so deep, that God's love is not deeper still." – Corrie Ten Boom (a Holocaust survivor)[23]

The English language only has one word for *love*, yet the Bible has four. The Hebrew word *hesed* refers to the unfailing, compassionate, covenant-keeping love of God. This kind of love endures, regardless of the response of the undeserving, unloving, stubbornness of the ones being loved. God loves without partiality of any kind. He doesn't force Himself on anyone, nor does He demand obedience. God's love forgives us thoroughly the first time we ask.

God created us with the need to love and be loved. Jesus said that loving God with all our heart, soul, and mind is the greatest commandment; and loving others as we love ourselves is the second greatest.[24] Jesus even tells us to love our enemies.[25] Love is important to God. Our notion of love is not pure, but His certainly is. His definition of love is extremely different from that of my culture: "Love is patient, love is kind. It does not envy, it does not boast, it is not proud. It does not dishonor others, it is not self-seeking, it is not easily angered, it keeps no record of wrongs. Love does not delight in evil but rejoices with the truth. It always protects, always trusts, always hopes, always perseveres. Love never fails."[26]

God doesn't just see our suffering; He enters into it with us. He moves toward us in our suffering. He is close to the brokenhearted.

Charles Spurgeon, a great English preacher from the 19th century, said in his sermon, *The Happy Christian*, something akin to, "God is too good to be cruel. He is too wise to be wrong; when you can't trace His hand, trust His heart."[27]

God's love for us is too deep to give us lesser things.

CHAPTER 10

A Game Changer
2016-2018

"There are no hopeless situations; there are only men who have grown hopeless about them."[28] Clare Boothe Luce

January 2016

In my upstream trek against the current of negativity, it was vital to keep speaking truth to myself. Biblical truth helped me live a meaningful life, despite my circumstances.

I fought hard to keep the lies out, though they continued to knock at my door. Healing was very important to me, but I didn't want it to be my life's primary ambition.

My top priority needed to be an ever-dependent, loving relationship with my Creator-God. After all, what can be seen is temporal, and what cannot be seen is eternal and of greater significance. That didn't mean I had stopped pursuing my goal for healing. No way! But it meant I needed to constantly evaluate my heart in all of this as I so often strayed.

As time passed, my hopes of resolution plummeted. At different times we tried to get help from Dr. Yao, a different pain management doctor, but there was no way to get in to see her when I was in a crisis. My physical therapist, Shari wanted a diagnosis before giving me more physical therapy. And my primary care physician didn't know what else to do for me.

Even though the orthopedic doctor didn't think the L5-S1 movement was excessive, this area was vulnerable from the extra torque caused by my SI fusions. I couldn't help but wonder if ligament laxity might once again be the culprit. So, I logged on to a prolotherapy web site. Immediately I noticed something new: stem cell therapy.

If you haven't heard much about regenerative medicine, you will. It's a game changer, with the potential to heal damaged tissues and organs of people who have conditions thought to be beyond repair.

In past decades, when I'd hear the term "stem cell," I would immediately think of those from an embryo. But different kinds of stem cells live all over our bodies: in our brain, bone marrow, blood, muscle, skin, heart, gut, liver, and even in our teeth!

The FDA states that these cell-based therapies are one of the most rapidly advancing approaches to repair, replace, restore, and regenerate cells, tissue, and organs. Bone marrow and organ transplants are examples of regenerative medicine that are already familiar to us.

Highly specialized cells from the heart, lung, and nerves, once thought unable to divide, are showing they possess some ability to self-heal with the help of regenerative medicine. Stem cells are the key component of regenerative medicine because of their ability to differentiate.

Stem cells can be taken from the body's bone marrow, blood, or fat and injected into tissue damaged by disease, injury, or aging. In theory, these stem cells transform into the kind of tissue needed to bring repair. It may be that my extensive and repeated injury depleted the cell structure's reservoir of healing agents. Perhaps introducing platelet-rich plasma and stem cells could dramatically increase my body's ability to heal itself!

The next time I saw the neurologist, I told him my theory: "If nothing shows up as a pain generator, then perhaps it is ligament laxity in the L5- S1 area." He said that sounded reasonable. I had had these thoughts early on, but because my pain was extremely severe and flare-ups lasted so much longer than my sacroiliac issues, I thought that something else was dreadfully wrong with me. Whatever was wrong, no one was seeing it — again! Unbelievable!

The neurologist was willing to refer me for stem cell therapy, but it turned out that I didn't need a referral. There were no insurance companies that covered this treatment because it was considered "investigational for musculoskeletal repair." I found a doctor who gave stem cell treatments and whose office was ten miles from our son's home in northern Philadelphia.

I was so hopeful that my stem cells would release healing agents and free me from this disabling pain. I had nothing to lose, except money. With an appointment just days away, I was about to burst! I had to simmer down because Tim doesn't like it when I put all my "eggs in one basket." Of course, he's the one who has to scrape me up off the pavement of disappointment when all the eggs in my basket break.

On February 1, 2016, I had my first adipose (fat) stem cell treatment. Hands down, it was the most painful treatment I have ever had! The liposuction, which was first, was nothing compared to what came next. Right before the doctor began injecting me with my stem cells, he handed me a ball to squeeze. I surely wish he had given me nitrous oxide instead.

From 2000 to 2004, I had hundreds and hundreds of injections deep into both large sacroiliac joint areas. I never looked at the size of the needle because I didn't want that image in my head. I knew that each time I went in for prolotherapy it was going to be painful. The temporary pain from those injections was nothing compared with the pain that I would experience if I didn't have them. Each time I had a treatment I told myself, *This is no big deal.* And it wasn't. However, this first stem cell treatment *was* a big deal.

At each main injection site, he gave several little squirts of the stem cell serum from various angles. When he finally finished, I sat up on the table and had a little cry; I was unnerved. I couldn't believe he hadn't at least sedated me. Why was blood splattered everywhere?

This doctor looked plumb worn out! Now I understood why he wore supports on his finger and thumb. He told me that he gives his own thumb stem cell treatments because of all the injections he administers. I don't know why, but at the end of the procedure, he gave me a paper photo of my derrière with the 32 main injection sights marked all around my sacroiliac joints.

Later, I thought: *Why in the world did he treat my SI area? It was fused; I wasn't having pain there! Why didn't he treat my low back where I told him* *my pain was? And for cryin' out loud, why didn't **I** think to question him when he started stabbing me in the buttock?* What a shame! What a waste!

It was no surprise that I didn't get good results from stem cell treatment because of the incorrect placement of the stem cells. But I wasn't ready give up on stem cell therapy. I did more research and found a place in Morristown, New Jersey, that uses Lipogems to process the stem cells.

How Lipogems work:
"Adipose tissue contains regenerative cells, growth factors, and healing proteins called cytokines. Cytokines are immune cells that signal other tissues to regenerate, repair, or heal. When adipose tissue is harvested, processed with the Lipogems technology, and injected into your injured tissues, it begins a cascade of immune responses that trigger cellular regeneration. As your cells repair, the cytokines also reduce inflammation in the area, which reduces pain and swelling, making your joints or soft tissues function better. Since Lipogems work on a cellular level, the healing process can take several weeks or months, but it doesn't prevent you from continuing your normal activities."[29]

Adipose stem cell treatments are given no closer than six months apart, which meant I had to wait until the end of July for the next attempt. In the meantime, I had two platelet-rich plasma (PRP) treatments and a prolotherapy treatment to hold me over until July.

Platelet Rich Plasma (PRP) Treatment:
*"Although blood is mainly a liquid (called plasma), it also contains small solid components (red cells, white cells, and platelets.)
The platelets are best known for their importance in clotting blood. However, platelets also contain hundreds of proteins called growth factors, which are very important in the healing of injuries.
PRP is plasma with many more platelets than what are typically found in the blood. The concentration of platelets — and, thereby, the concentration of growth factors — can be 5 to 10 times richer than usual. In preparation for PRP, blood must first be drawn from the patient. The platelets are separated from other blood cells, and their*

concentration is increased during a process called centrifugation. Then the increased concentration of platelets is combined with the remaining blood."[30]

The next month Julie gave birth to our tenth grandchild. Levi bounded into this world with three adoring sisters to greet him. I've always said that I would have loved to see my husband as a child. Well, Levi gives me that image; he certainly looks like his Poshie. And like his Poshie, he always makes me laugh.

Just before the publishing of this book, Jonathan and Jolie adopted a precious brother and sister, Leo and Roslyn. Six grandsons and six granddaughters, each of inestimable value, knit together by our Creator and placed into our family to love and point to Jesus. This whole world called "grandparenting" that they opened up to me was better than anything I could have ever imagined!

Tim noticed that when the grandkids came in the front door, my mind went out the back. I would only think with my heart. My "protect yourself" mindset went on the back burner until they left. Therefore, Tim watched out for me even more carefully when they were around. I am completely in love with my grandkids and want to make the most of the time I spend with them. They are the best-ever distraction from pain and gloom.

There certainly is a time and place for distraction when you live in chronic pain. Physical and emotional pain usually feels worse at night because the activity and noise around us subsides. There is less noise available to drown out all the painful messages going to the brain. But if distractions override beneficial pain signals and common sense, then the distractions end up doing us more harm than good.

I hate the commercial where someone is painting a ceiling, develops pain, takes a pill, and goes right back to painting the ceiling. Something is very wrong with that picture! What's worse is that it sets a precedent for the viewers.

July 29th was the day of my adipose stem cell treatment in New Jersey. It was a cakewalk compared to that first brutal stem cell treatment.

My doctor used the Lipogems device to process my adipose tissue, extracted through liposuction. With guided fluoroscopy, he accurately injected that "liquid gold" into my lower back region between the L5-S1 area. The results were absolutely amazing; this treatment was a game changer!

I built up my muscles by swimming laps. In no time at all, I was functioning again! Two months after the Lipogems treatment, I was well enough to care for my grandchildren for 40 hours a week. God's timing was impeccable! The very month Jessica began her new job, I was healed enough to care for Elijah and Raven, then two and three years old!

Unknown to me, the year before, my neurologist was suspicious of multiple sclerosis. Now a year later, in December, I had another MRI, following up on my brain lesion. Thankfully there was no change and no multiple sclerosis! However, my health had declined, and I needed more help.

A year later on October 18, 2017:

Dear Holly,

Since summer, I've seen subtle signs of sliding backward. But now it's obvious that I need another adipose stem cell treatment for my back. I've been down, as in barely functioning. But still, I'm better now than I was before I had the stem cell treatment, as I can still get myself a drink. In this past year, I've only had a few flare-ups that lasted just a few days, using just Tylenol and the TENS, no narcotics! I was thrilled when I learned that Tim was all in favor of another stem cell treatment. (If only they weren't so expensive.) I'm extremely thankful that we've found a treatment that works and have enough money for it! I am counting the days — just eight more.

Love,

Kerri

I had my next adipose stem cell treatment the end of October. When I mentioned to the doctor that I was also having pain in my hips, he injected some stem cells into both hips at no extra charge.

Again, I saw tremendous results from the stem cells. In just a couple of weeks, I was back in the game. I was so thankful to be living in a time and place where I had access to these regenerative procedures. Although science has begun discovering regenerative processes, our Creator-God has known all this from the beginning. He placed these healing capabilities within Adam when He formed him from the dust of the ground and breathed life into his nostrils.

He already knew Adam and Eve would choose to disobey and live under sin's curse. But out of His goodness, He provided a means for these dying bodies to know limited healing. Imagine if every injury or sickness we've ever had didn't heal. Few would be able to get out of bed in the morning. God is good.

The year 2018 went much like the year before; my back held up great, just a few manageable bumps on the road that only needed a few days of rest. But when autumn arrived, I encountered yet another major back flare-up. We made plans for my fourth stem cell treatment.

What would cause us to want to spend our thin savings on a temporary fix? Non-negotiable, incapacitating, relentless pain! We had found nothing other than stem cell treatments to help. We didn't know what else to do. These treatments seemed to be keeping me out of bed for a year at a time.

Our Monday night Bible study group decided to have a golf ball drop fundraiser for us. People purchased a numbered golf ball. One windy, rainy fall Sunday, our good friends, the Watts, hosted the event. Cleon flew his helicopter over a flagged hole and dropped all the golf balls. The owners of the three closest golf balls to the flag got monetary prizes. In just three weeks, they raised $4,500. We were overwhelmed; it was enough to pay for the whole treatment! What a generous expression of love from friends and strangers, to share this financial burden with us! You can only imagine what an encouragement that was, especially in light of what happened next.

The much-anticipated treatment did not help at all. Six weeks later, I was still in bed. Why? Was it the spondylolisthesis? Autonomic nervous system dysfunction? Cellular depletion? What should I do now? I didn't know where to turn. But I couldn't turn to despair. I had to remember and apply all that I'd been learning along the way. And recall the encouragement I had gleaned from some great role models. I'd like to share a few of them with you.

Eric, the grandson of a dear friend, once wrote to me:

> *If ever you wonder if you can make it through a challenge, please remember what God has done for me, enabling me to have joy in the midst of what without Him would be sorrow. Because of Him, I am GRATEFUL that I have been paralyzed. And I have known more joy than probably any year before. If God can do this in my life, with my weaknesses, faults, and problems, He can surely do this in anyone else's life that allows Him to.*

Making the most of their pitiful suffering, Corrie Ten Boom and her sister Betsy held Bible studies for their fellow inmates during their imprisonment at Germany's Ravensbruck Concentration Camp. Upon meeting her cruelest of former prison guards years later, Corrie stretched out her hand to pronounce to the man, "I forgive you, brother, with all my heart."[31]

Prompting her action was the forgiveness she had first received from Jesus. Corrie said she had never known God's love as intensely as she did at that moment, realizing it was not her love, but the power of God within her. An abundance of inner joy followed as a result of her obedient posture before God. Speaking to millions through her book, *Tramp for the Lord*, her movie, *The Hiding Place*, and countless talks to audiences around the world, she allowed God to use her experiences of grievous suffering to encourage others in their affliction.

Nick Vujicic is one of seven people worldwide known to have Phocomelia (no arms and no legs). He questioned the purpose of life and if his life even had a purpose. But hope began to dawn at the age of fifteen when he was reading from John chapter nine in his Bible. People were asking Jesus why the man before them was born blind. They wanted to know if he was blind because of his sin or the sin of his parents. Jesus said that he was blind "so that the works of God might be displayed in him."[32]

Upon reading that, Nick decided to trust God's plan for his life. In Nick's own words: "I said to God that if He had a plan for that man, I certainly believed He had one for me. I totally surrendered the 'needing to know the plan' and trusted in Him one day at a time."[33]

He found a deep peace in knowing that God had good intentions for his life. He stopped blaming God and started trusting that He was up to something good.

At the young age of twenty-three, he founded the international non-profit ministry called "Life Without Limbs." This platform allowed him to share his perspective on life, lead a campaign against bullying, and, most dear to his heart, offer his audience the good news of Jesus Christ.

Though Nick and his gorgeous wife live in California with their four beautiful children, he travels! He has spoken to more than 830 million people in 69 different countries. I wrote down these words from one of his talks I listened to on YouTube: "It's been said that doors open to a man without arms and legs much more easily than to anyone else. I thank God for providing that privilege!"[34]

Struggling with deep depression but wanting to trust God, Joni Eareckson Tada asked her friend Steve Estes an honest question: "If God allowed my accident to happen at such a young age, an accident that left me a quadriplegic, then what might He do next?"

Steve replied with powerful wisdom. "Joni, God permits what He hates, to accomplish what He loves." She said that little phrase was jam-packed with so much meaning it set the course for the rest of her life.

Steve continued to explain: "Joni, God allows all sorts of things He doesn't approve of. God hated the torture, injustice, and treason that led to the crucifixion (of Jesus). Yet He permitted it so that the world's worst murder could become the world's only salvation. In the same way, God hates spinal cord injury, He permitted it for the sake of Christ in you, as well as others."[35]

On the 50th anniversary of her diving accident, Joni said, "What a difference time makes — as well as prayer, heaven-minded friends, and deep study of God's Word. All combined, I began to see there are more important things in life than walking and having use of your hands. It sounds incredible, but I really would rather be in this wheelchair knowing Jesus as I do than be on my feet without him."[36]

Joni is a daily inspiration for millions. She has authored over 50 books, recorded several musical albums, and starred in an autobiographical movie. She has delivered a four-minute inspirational daily broadcast for more than four decades, founded Wheels for the World (distributing wheelchairs to impoverished individuals worldwide), and established Family Retreats, serving, as Joni says, "a slice of heaven" for families of disabilities in a camp environment.

Because Eric, Corrie, Nick, and Joni all have great attitudes toward their suffering, they are stellar examples to me of how to make the most of my suffering. God has been accomplishing His good purposes in their lives because they chose to wrestle through the challenging theological issues, trust God, and allow Him to use their disabilities. Their good attitudes didn't come without struggle; and their good attitudes will not be without great reward!

But Jesus is my greatest role model in suffering. He wants me to adopt His attitude, values, and perspectives in every circumstance. The Bible tells me to have the same mindset He had: "When they hurled their insults at him, he did not retaliate; when he suffered, he made no threats. Instead, he entrusted himself to him who judges justly."[37]

While Jesus undeservedly hung on that Roman cross, He talked with John about his mother's care, gave assurance to a repentant thief, and prayed for his persecutors. What a powerful example of caring for others when His needs were off the charts!

A Closer Look at THOROUGH GOODNESS

> "We don't have the capacity to exaggerate God's goodness.
> We can distort it, or even misrepresent it,
> but we can never exaggerate it."
> Bill Johnson[38]

I can do good things and have good character traits, but God is good *in essence*. He is infinitely kind and full of goodwill toward us. God is not good when all is going great for me today and bad if my world is rocked by catastrophe tomorrow. He is not the author of evil. Evil is the absence of goodness and the result of man's rebellion toward God. My soul can rest knowing that God's overarching plan for me is good although my circumstances may be evil. Even what my enemy means to use to destroy me, God uses for my good! When bad things happen and I cannot perceive His goodness, the future will display the grandeur of His plans; they are always good because He is good!

CHAPTER 11

Suffering Redeemed
AROUND A.D. 30

I believe we all yearn for the respect and approval of others. Around the globe, the wealthy are automatically esteemed because of their homes, cars, and clothes. Hardworking athletes are honored for their strength and diligence, even if they don't win. The intellectual only needs to open his mouth for a few minutes before he earns the admiration of his listeners. But what about the valiant efforts and patient perseverance of society's sufferers? They run their race to the best of their ability, yet no one stands by with a trophy for them. Even more than regard for their daily courage, however, I think debilitated victims crave purpose in their affliction. I think they long for their suffering to be redeemed. *I do!*

There are many definitions for the word *redeem*: buy back, deliver, emancipate, liberate, make good, make up for, ransom, restore, save, and win back.

We all love redemptive stories birthed out of the womb of affliction. I want redemptive value to come from my pain just as much as the next guy. But I can't pound out a purpose or beat benevolence out of all this pain any more than I can make it go away. Anything positive or redemptive is beyond my imagination and ability to ensue. But from reading the Bible, I've found that God specializes in these kinds of situations. He is the Lord of Redemption; that's His specialty.

Penned by forty very different authors under the inspiration of God's Spirit, the Bible recounts an overarching unified story of God's pursuit to redeem humanity and restore us to a loving relationship with Him. The Bible tells me of the greatest redemptive story of all time.

The first chapter of the first book, Genesis, says that God created everything and said that it was all "very good." Suffering in this world was not His intent. So where did it originate?

Sometime before creating earth and after creating the angelic realm, God's anointed guardian cherub, full of wisdom and perfect in beauty, became filled with the pride of his position, beauty, and splendor. He no longer wanted to serve but desired to be served — to be divine. We know that God gave these spiritual beings free will because some of them followed this rebellious cherub, resulting in their expulsion from God's presence.

Of all creation, only humans were stamped in the Creator's image, purposed to reflect His flawless character. God delighted in Adam and Eve and provided them with the unimaginable goodness of Eden. With just one restriction, not to eat from the tree in the center of the garden, God gave people the freedom to love Him. He didn't want programmed robots.

With the ability to disguise himself as an intelligent talking creature, that enemy cherub of God set out to allure mankind to jump on his bandwagon and join his revolt. This adversary tempted Eve with the concept of being her own boss and with the idea that God really wasn't good.

Adam and Eve both chose to reject God's authority and disobeyed His one and only rule. All the pristine beauty and harmony of the original creation shattered. God had told Adam that the punishment for disobedience would be death. God couldn't look the other way and ignore their disobedience. His justice demanded retribution.

Much like a plant cut from its roots, Adam and Eve were cut off from their source of life. Now a marred image of their Creator, they were no longer righteous.

Since kind begets kind, Adam and Eve's children would inherently be corrupt. No one ever had to teach me how to be selfish or lie. No, my parents had to work very hard to instruct me to the contrary: to love, to be patient, to share, and to give. I understood from an early age that my natural bent was to do wrong, all the time!

Because even when I produce a string of good works, a steady flow of wrong motives streams right through them.

Growing up, I learned from the Old Testament that people cannot approach God on their terms. God choose to reveal Himself to the nation of Israel and taught them that they had to come to Him in the way that He said — with ritual washing and a lamb free of blemish to sacrifice. The sacrificial system taught the Israelites that they were not fit for His presence and that there was a required payment due for their offenses.

We understand reconciliation is a legal matter; society needs civil laws to live in peace. If someone were to kidnap my grandchild and return that child a month later saying, "Oh, there's no problem, officer, because I'm sorry," that just wouldn't fly. There must be restitution for failing to treat others with the same respect we desire.

To a much greater and more serious degree, we can't sin against God and get away with it. We can't treat Him as less than who He is and then just say, "Sorry."

Words apart from reparation don't make amends. The Bible teaches that I have no way of making restitution with God; I have no righteousness or good works that God will accept. Repeatedly, the Bible teaches that the payment for our sin is death. However, there is very good news! Even before God created man, He had devised a plan to satisfy the need for justice without denying His tenacious love and mercy for the people He would create. God made a way to redeem us.

God told the ancient Israelites to put their hand on an unblemished lamb before sacrificing it, signifying that they agreed with God that their sin debt required death. The lamb experienced their death by proxy. These sacrifices continued year after year until the Messiah, the Lamb of God, came to earth.

Who exactly is this Lamb of God? Jesus Christ, God in flesh and bones. Because of the things He claimed about Himself, Jesus couldn't be just another prophet. He taught that He alone forgives sin and is the only way to a restored relationship with God.

However, when their Messiah did come, the Israelites were looking for deliverance from the oppression of Rome, not from their true oppressors: sin, Satan, and death. Only after the death and resurrection of Jesus were they able to understand that He came to earth the first time as their Suffering Servant, to pay their sin debt. Now there is no longer a need to put lambs to death because Jesus, the Lamb of God, took the punishment we deserve on Himself. His resurrection from the dead brought redemption for those who want it!

There is no sitting on this fence. I would either be God's forgiven child or His enemy. I made the decision early in my life to become His child, a decision I've never regretted. When I applied the death of Jesus to my sinful heart as a child, it was as though I placed my hand on Jesus (not a symbolic animal), acknowledging that He suffered death to ransom me and remove my sin and shame. It all boiled down to what I believed: either I believed what the Bible said about Jesus, or I took matters into my own hands and lived apart from Him.

What compels me to believe this masterpiece of manuscripts, this story that I've heard thousands of times since I was knee-high to a grasshopper? Is it that the cohesive, intriguing message was written over a span of 1,500 years, that the tiniest details of some sixty major prophecies were fulfilled in Jesus the Christ, that the Dead Sea scrolls confirm biblical accuracy, that ten of Jesus' closest followers were willing to be martyred for His name's sake (people don't do that sort of thing for a dead man), that it was miraculously preserved (though viciously opposed and oppressed) over millennia, that millions and millions of lives down through the centuries have been completely transformed by its message, and that it has authenticity in my own life? Yes! Yes! Yes!

But the heart of the matter was the matter of my heart! Repentance is a change of mind, making a 180-degree turn from independence to dependence on God's words. Repentance wasn't an act of my salvation, but rather a result of it. I could have never cleaned up my act to come to God. Rather, after I had a true change of heart, He began transforming my brokenness. I was cleansed to enter into a meaningful, loving relationship with my Creator. Forgiveness was not an end, but a means to an end, to eternal intimacy with the Almighty!

As Jesus hung on that cruel Roman cross, God's justice, hatred of sin, and depth of love were displayed. What God had planned before creating the world came to fruition because He longed for each one of us to have a loving relationship with Him.

"For God [the greatest power] *so loved the world* [His greatest creation] *that He gave His One and only Son* [the greatest gift] *that whosoever believeth on Him* [the greatest opportunity] *should not perish* [the

greatest pardon] *but have everlasting life* [the greatest provision] (John 3:16)."

The results of receiving God's redemption are extensive and marvelous! The moment I obtained God's forgiveness, I was adopted into God's family and given a new identity. Just as children usually have characteristics and mannerisms of their parents, so my Father began His good work within me. He began the long process of transforming my character so I can better reflect His.

Though I'm a work in progress, I have a wholly restored relationship with Him and full access to talk with Him anywhere and anytime! I'm the object of His passionate, tender care and unconditional, eternal love, free to live my life based on who God says I am, rather than how I feel! And I now have peace *with* God and the peace *of* God!

Because the God of all living things is meeting my needs, I'm free to pursue relationships for what I can give rather than what I can get out of them. With His love and compassion flowing through me, I'll want to move toward people. Because I've received His complete forgiveness, I have a basis from which to forgive others. The Spirit of God urges me to offer this redemptive story of our suffering Jesus to the broken humanity around me. His Spirit motivated me to write this memoir as a means to share the greatest redemption story of all time!

I had a surreal moment in the doctor's office on my first trip to Atlanta, Georgia. After 12 years of mere bandage solutions for my debilitating pain, I finally had answers as to what was generating my back pain and a plan for restoration. But just the discovery of what was wrong was not enough; I had to take action. I had to have the surgery to enjoy freedom from pain.

So, it is with this message of God's redemption. Giving mental assent to the fact that Jesus died on a cross and rose three days later doesn't make restitution for my sin. I had to take action and agree with God about my sin and respond in belief to what God said about His Son paying my debt. Much as I do when I put my faith in a chair to hold me up when I sit in it, I took my seat in Jesus, fully trusting in Him alone, not any "good works" of my own.

When I responded to God's redemption, telling Him that I wanted the death of Jesus applied to me, my words and understanding were rudimentary for I was a child. But it was real. Immediately after, I felt an immense joy about my decision. Not everyone does, and that's okay. It's not about a feeling but rather about trusting. And God knew that He had won my heart!

The Bible says that it's not the healthy who need a doctor, but the sick. In other words, only those willing to admit they are sinners will ever need a Savior. Are you fed up with bandage solutions to your debilitating sin condition? Are you ready for a surreal moment with the One your soul has been searching for? As I've been writing this memoir, I've been praying for you to know Him. I long for you to know Him!

God knows your pain, your anger, and your secrets, and none of that drives Him away. You are both fully known and fully loved. He's not angry at you; He's passionately pursuing you. He Who is whole was utterly broken so that we who are utterly broken can become completely whole. **Whole-ly broken**!

The crucifixion proved that God would go all-out to redeem our broken relationship. But right now, a critical battle is waged on our soul's front. Will we surrender to God and allow Him to fix our spiritual brokenness and become wholly His?

God is allowing evil to play out in the world because He is patiently waiting for people to turn to Him. It seems to me that God is not very involved where He is not welcomed. He never forces Himself on us; rather He knocks, invites, and waits to be welcomed into our lives. But He will not wait indefinitely. There is a day of reckoning coming. Therefore, today is the day to open your heart's door to Him.

Minutes before Jesus left this earth and was taken into heaven, He told his disciples to take His message of redemption to all nations, making it clear that God wants *all* ethnicities to hear and respond to His provision of a restored life.

I grew up seeing photos and hearing stories of isolated people groups tucked away in the far corners of the world. In my early teen years, these presentations stirred me. I wanted to do something about making Jesus known where He has never been heard of before.

That is why Tim and I lived in Venezuela. We were part of a team working together to help the twenty-six indigenous people groups in Venezuela have the opportunity to hear God's plan for their redemption.

In the last book of the Bible, the apostle John spoke about having a glimpse into heaven and seeing people from "every tribe, language, people, and nation" around God's throne.[39] God doesn't want anyone to miss out on his rescue plan. He wants relationship with everyone!

A Closer Look at TRUTH and JUSTICE

I believe that "While many things can *have* the truth, only one thing can *be* the truth, with that one thing being God Himself."[40] People who say, "There is no truth" are declaring that concept to be their truth and are contradicting themselves.

Without justice, there is no liberty. Without truth, there is no justice. God is the plumb line for truth, which His justice carries out. What I think is right or wrong doesn't matter; I'm not qualified to set the standard. Truth emanates from our unchanging God. His justice is not only fair; it is right and good, even in sentencing evil.

American pastor and author of the last century, A.W. Tozer shared his thoughts on this subject saying, "God spares us because He is good, but He could not be good if He were not just. Through the work of Christ in atonement, justice is not violated but satisfied when God spares a sinner. … Every wrathful judgment in the history of the world has been a holy act of preservation. The holiness of God, the wrath of God, and the health of His creation are inseparably united. God's wrath is His utter intolerance of whatever degrades and destroys."[41]

When I know the truth, I'm less likely to fall for a lie. Jesus said, "I am the way and the truth and the life. No one comes to the Father except through me."[42] There is no other way. I'm thankful that I'm not worrying, crossing my fingers, and wondering if I'm going to make it to the Father.

CHAPTER 12

Useless Pain
2018-2020

"Pain protects us from destroying ourselves. Yet I also know that pain itself can destroy."[43] Dr. Paul Brand

Struggling with pain and all those unanswered questions I had as to why that last stem cell treatment didn't help, I decided to go back to Shari for physical therapy. After examining me and listening well, she was convinced that the majority of my problem was something called central sensitization. She seized my attention when she said that she thought about 80% of my current issues stemmed from it. We spent the rest of that appointment talking about central sensitization. This problem was not "all in my head" as the cliché goes. In reality, the breakdown was indeed happening in my head and spine, where my nerve receptors were overreacting. I left my time with her feeling somewhat shell-shocked, learning that I'd been receiving faulty pain signals. Being told that I couldn't trust my pain sensors was like telling me that I couldn't believe my eyes to tell me what I was seeing. My back, where I felt all the pain, was not the main culprit. Overactive pain signals were to blame; they were hijacking my life!

In a nutshell, my chronic pain was responsible for rewiring my nervous system. My brain was not getting a report on the *actual* state of my tissues; instead, it was getting the *opinion* of my central nervous system. My brain perceived way more pain than what made sense for the condition of my tissue. There was nothing wrong with my nervous system, as there was nothing wrong with its "hardware." However, there was a glitch in my "software" program, continually reporting "danger" to my nervous system.

> *After repeated stimulation, neurotransmitters and electrical signals create brain changes. Neurons develop a "memory" for responding to these signals. The more frequent the stimulation (or pain episodes), the stronger the brain memory becomes. In turn, the brain will respond more rapidly and effectively when the next flare-up hits. "A super-sensitive nervous system and immune cells (called 'glia') release chemicals which 'turn up the volume,' increasing the number of connections and signals whizzing around the brain and spinal cord.*[44]
>
> *"Long considered to be little more than cellular glue holding the brain together, glia, which outnumbers neurons 10 to 1, are now appreciated as critical contributors to the health of the central nervous system, with recognized roles in the formation of synapses, neuronal plasticity, and protection against neurodegeneration. Research has demonstrated that glia seems to respond and adapt to the cumulative danger signals that can result from different kinds of injury and illness, and that they appear to prime neural pathways for the over activation that causes persistent pain."*[45]

This is why my flare-ups didn't make any sense. For example, one time I was lying on my side while reading stories to my two young grandchildren. Attempting to see the picture, one of them accidentally bumped my back with his knee which did not cause an actual injury. However, my nervous system translated that bump as highly offensive and started a chain reaction which quickly set off a dynamic inflammation response to protect my "injury." Surprisingly, it took me six weeks to recover from that little bump.

As the cumulative years of chronic pain rolled by, my brain got better and better at detecting and reporting pain. It sent louder and louder messages to get my attention. Pain-free activity lessened, making me more and more disabled. With central sensitization, even discomfort can creep in from merely feeling threatened or anxious about pain.

> Melanie Themstrom says in her book <u>The Pain Chronicle</u> that "chronic pain often outlives its original causes, worsens over time, and takes on a puzzling life of its own ... There is increasing evidence that over time, untreated pain eventually rewrites the central nervous system, causing pathological changes to the brain and spinal cord and that these, in turn, cause greater pain. Even more disturbingly, recent evidence suggests that prolonged pain actually damages parts of the brain, including those involved in cognition."[46]

Sadly, central sensitization was not on the radar of any of the doctors that I saw. There are no clear criteria for diagnosing central sensitization; no lab tests or checklist can confirm it, making it very easy for sufferers to slip through the cracks.

No doubt, central sensitization was why my fight-and-flight response stayed revved up. Maybe that's why the over-the-counter pain medication never helped, and narcotics never did enough. In light of all this new information, my long bouts of exacerbated pain were finally beginning to make sense!

Central sensitization could be an aspect of any chronic pain situation, but not necessarily the complete cause, as pain could still be coming from a continuing problem in the tissue or structure. I have too much movement between my last vertebra and my sacrum, so some portion of my pain probably comes from that. This may explain why the stem cell treatments were helpful for a time, strengthening my low back connective tissue, significantly lessening the trigger response for flare-ups, but only for a season.

I'm so thankful Shari knew about central sensitization. She told me about Professor Lorimer Moseley, a pain scientist from Australia. I listened to many of his talks on YouTube to learn about this condition. According to Moseley, pain is a protector, *not* an accurate measure of tissue health. Tissue can be completely safe, but my system can involuntarily fire messages of being threatened and endangered. Our pain networking system can lose its capacity to be specific and precise, making our pain non-informative and unhelpful. The system my Designer provided to protect me had become counterproductive.

With central sensitization, pain alarms keep on ringing, much like the phantom pain of an amputee. Useless pain! Just when everything was looking so bleak to me, Shari interjected some great news: neuroplasticity!

Neuroplasticity:
"With every repetition of a thought or emotion, we reinforce a neural pathway — and with each new thought, we begin to create a new way of being. These small changes, frequently enough repeated, lead to changes in how our brains work. Neuroplasticity is the 'muscle building' part of the brain; the things we do often, we become stronger at, and what we don't use fades away. That is the physical basis of why making a thought or action over and over again increases its power. Over time, it becomes automatic, a part of us. We literally become what we think and do."[47]

Because of the malleability of our brain, central sensitization can be reversed. Professor Mosely's website, tamethebeast.org, explains what feeds the beast of central sensitization and what tames it. He believes that with time, effort, and understanding, you can retrain your faulty pain warning system.

I read that cultivating a healthy balance of avoidance and exposure is foundational for recovery. Avoidance is about making life safer, avoiding the stress that sets things off. Exposure is doing everything possible to keep moving. A balance of the two is supposed to give me confidence that what I'm doing is safe.

SAFE:
"When your CNS (central nervous system) is 'freaked out' and over-interpreting every signal from the tissues as more painful than

> *it should, therapy becomes more about soothing yourself and feeling safe than about fixing tissues. Pain is, at a very fundamental level, all about your brain's assessment of safety: unsafe things hurt. If your brain thinks you're safe, pain goes down."*[48]

Avoidance and exposure sound logical on paper. Despite trying to balance those two things for years, I was unsuccessful. All I did was rebound into pain. These explanations made sense, but knowledge alone was not enough to change things. Hopefully, as pain science advances, there will be more help available for recalibrating the central nervous system.

Pain is tricky. Boundaries of what I could and could not do safely changed continuously. In the early years of my physical therapy, I spent a lot of time stretching, and then later I was told not to stretch. Sometimes a long soak in a hot tub with Epsom salts helped a lot; other times, a hot tub made my pain worse. There were times I could challenge myself physically and swim a few extra laps; other times, it bit me in the butt to even kick my legs a tiny bit. For decades, I benefitted greatly from using my TENS unit, but I didn't use it until my pain was at a level four. Since learning about central sensitization, I discovered that I had much better results when I began using the device at the inception of pain, rather than waiting until things escalated. Decades ago, I was told not to take pain medication to do more physical activity; I should be in bed if I needed muscle relaxants or narcotics. But when I learned that central sensitization was my issue, I was told that at the first sign of trouble, I should aggressively smother the pain with medication, as you would a small flame before it quickly became a forest fire.

The body is so interconnected that one significant issue affects other body members. My back issue began thirty years ago as a ligament problem which ultimately led to this neurological flaw. Over time, circulatory, digestive, endocrine, muscular, neurological, psychological, and urinary issues developed all because the connective tissues in my pelvis didn't do their job. One of the first spiritual lessons I learned from my suffering was realizing that my SI joint was representative of me in the body of Christ. The Bible teaches that followers of Jesus Christ are members of one body, of which Jesus is the head. When I am not doing my part to serve, my dysfunction has profound effects on the rest of the body. Can you imagine trying to eat your dinner with an elbow that refuses to bend? Every single member of the body of Christ needs to be functioning, as God intends. If I choose to be idle and irresponsible, I'm a detriment to all of the other members.

Shari felt that I needed additional help in managing my condition, as her training was strictly in physical rehabilitation. You can only imagine how happy I was to learn from her that there was now a new pain management doctor in town!

This new pain management doctor suggested revisiting the spinal cord stimulator. Several things had changed since my spinal cord stimulator trial five years previous. I now had a diagnosis (central sensitization), kidneys were fine, and I learned that there was another kind of stimulator available that did not require a laminectomy (the removal of some vertebral bone fragments). Since spinal cord stimulators are for patients with unhelpful and unnecessary pain, I was on board. I signed up for the required trial stimulator as soon as they could get me in.

They ran thin leads along the epidural space in the spinal cord and used three rolls of tape to secure the battery pack to the outside of my body. Well, maybe not three full rolls, but it felt like it. I had great results with the five-day trial stimulator. I then had to wait the necessary time for things to heal internally before the permanent implant surgery could be done. I had every reason to believe this was going to help. And the spinal cord stimulator was a complete success! I enjoyed the freedom of social outings, grocery shopping, and doing things with my family. In fact, I felt well enough to sit up to work on this book. When my back started to hurt, I could lie down and rest for 20-30 minutes and get back up feeling fine. The vortex of pain was gone!

Just weeks after the permanent spinal cord stimulator was implanted, I learned that the lead on the right side had migrated, making that lead ineffective. (The leads connect with specific nerves to block the pain.) But I still received sufficient relief from the left lead.

A year later, I was wrapping up this book with my editor, thinking that my journey with pain was well under control. Then just two days before Christmas, I succumbed to a horrible back flare-up that dragged on and on. Shortly after I got back on my feet, I had yet another flare-up. I thought something else had gone terribly wrong with my back. I waited for weeks on end to have an MRI on a special machine because of my spinal stimulator. Then a week before my appointment we were told that because the lead had migrated to the lumbar area, where I was now having pain, the MRI was not permitted. The metal in the lead threatened to damage their imaging machine. Finally, in May, we learned from a simple x-ray that now the left lead had moved as well. Three months later, my 72nd healthcare provider, whom I had seen for my back pain, was able to replace the whole system with a new spinal cord stimulator with anchored leads. Thankfully, I was once again functioning.

Sadly, before the final touches of this book were completed, I spent seven weeks in bed with back pain and eight more weeks trying to get back on my feet. Clearly my saga isn't over. Life as I know it can be turned upside down in a flash. Every hour of every day is uncertain for all of us. Although I don't know how many more chapters lie ahead, I know that my future is bright.

The light at the end of the tunnel is not the healing of physical pain, as I used to believe. The light at the end of the tunnel is the same Light who is present with me in the middle: Jesus. When I anchor my purpose for living, joy, security, or comfort in something temporary, then I'm always at risk of losing it. I'd never choose to go through any of this, but I sure wouldn't want to be without all that I have learned through it. Affliction was the catalyst that grew my trust in God. Although I've said, "God has taught me that He can be trusted," the truth is, at the dawn of each new day, I need to choose to trust God in every new set of circumstances. Hopefully, with stronger faith, I'll be slower to doubt and quicker to believe Him.

In 1996, God did not come through for me as I had expected; I felt desolate. It seemed as though God were hiding from me, like some sick game of hide-n-seek. For all my life, I believed in the goodness of God, but in that dark pit of despair, I doubted His love for me. Intense suffering *will* bring doubts and fears to the surface. But just because dark storm clouds hide the sun doesn't mean it's not shining. How I perceive God may change because of my changing chemistry and fluctuating feelings, but that doesn't alter Who He is or the promises He has made. The world around me is changing fast, as is my aging body, but God's character is the *one* thing that cannot change! It anchors me when the tempest rages.

When I doubt God, I don't believe Him. Disbelieving God implies that He's a liar, that He's not able, that His goodness isn't good enough, or that He's not trustworthy. It's as if I'm bringing God into my courtroom and finding Him less than what He said He is. When I do that, I'm casting judgment without complete evidence. I see such a tiny piece of the picture, while God sees it all. Blaming God for my pain is wrong thinking. He did not create evil; He allowed for choice. At the root of accusing God that He is not good or fair was the thinking that I could make better choices than God. But I can't! The truth is, I am not qualified to make those kinds of calls, but God is.

My options are to trust self, others, or God. We humans are limited in every way and fallible in every aspect of our beings: belittling, criticizing, disrespecting, impatient, lying, misjudging, slandering, stealing, taking advantage of, undisciplined, unfaithful, unkind, and extremely selfish! In every aspect of God's essence, He is infallible, incapable of error. He has never messed up, nor ever will, not even once!

In light of God's character, I ask: Is He trustworthy? Will I trust Him when I am mad with pain? When there is no hope in sight? When it seems illogical or pointless? When, yet again, my heart is broken? When it seems I'm not getting anything out of trusting Him? Observing His magnificent creation shows me His unmatched wisdom and unlimited resources. Therefore, it makes sense to trust Him implicitly.

When it's settled in my mind that God is trustworthy, I have courage, assurance, rest, and joy. I'll take *courage* knowing that Jehovah of the Old and New Testaments is the same One at work in my life today. Anchored to God, I am not in jeopardy of losing my identity or my purpose for living. And when He takes something away that I treasure, I'm *assured* that it's not because He doesn't love me.

Trusting God in the middle of suffering means I'll be confident that God allows what He hates in order to accomplish what He loves and that His good intentions are bigger and better than anything I could dream up. I am at *rest* comparing the size of what I'm facing against the sufficiency of the Almighty!

My antidote for worry, fear, doubt, anxiety, and lack of confidence is knowing and believing in the essence of who God is. He is a reservoir of comfort and peace. And *joy* will be the result of a proper response to God's character, regardless of my circumstances.

Regardless (Written in 1997)
- *Regardless of what bad thing clobbers me today, God is good through and through.*
- *Regardless of what I think of what He permits, God is just in all He does.*
- *Regardless of whether God does something that seems wrong to me, He is completely righteous.*
- *Regardless of whether I am pouting or bitter, God is faithful.*
- *Regardless of what I choose to believe about God, He doesn't make mistakes.*
- *Regardless of whether God seems loving, He is love.*
- *Regardless of how I perceive Him today, God is Who He is.*

In parenting my children, sometimes my instructions, advice, and warnings were useless without some form of suffering to help convince my kids that what I was saying was pertinent. God, the perfect parent, can't just leave me to myself because my character is really important to Him. Good parenting comes from good discipline. Discipline comes from the word *disciple*. *Disciple* comes from the Latin word *discipulus* meaning *student*. Discipline comes in three forms: preventative, supportive, and corrective. In love, God disciples me because I belong to Him.

"The Lord disciplines the ones He loves, and He chastens everyone He accepts as His son. Endure hardship as discipline; God is treating you as His children. For what children are not disciplined by their father? If you are not disciplined — and everyone undergoes discipline — then you are not legitimate, not true sons and daughters at all. Moreover, we have all had human fathers who disciplined us, and we respected them for it. How much more should we submit to the Father of spirits and live! They disciplined us for a little while as they thought best; but God disciplines us for our good, so that we may share in His holiness. No discipline seems pleasant at the time, but painful. Later on, however, it produces a harvest of righteousness and peace for those who have been trained by it." Hebrews 12:6-11

The vehicle of pain and suffering has transferred a lot of my head knowledge down into my heart, the core of my being, where transformation takes place. King David, the psalmist wrote: "It was good for me to be afflicted so that I might learn Your decrees."[49] He also said, "Before I was afflicted, I went astray, but now I obey your word."[50]

At times, in the throes of pain, all I focused on was getting out of it; yet, at other times, I leaned into it enough to learn from it. God gives us the freedom to choose to learn or to be bitter. The results are polarizing.

Nothing reveals character like pain and suffering, and nothing can build faith and strength of character like pain and suffering. As a muscle grows from lifting weights, so the resistance of trials allows the muscles of faith to grow. I have prayed and asked God to grow my faith many times without considering what it would take to do that.

Centuries of human experience and Scripture affirm that God has limited much of His working to our asking. God *can* accomplish His will without our praying; He doesn't need our help. But it seems as if God often limits His involvement to our invitation. According to the Bible, even our character may influence God's activity: "The prayer of a righteous person is powerful and effective." [51]

Back in 1993, after two years of unsuccessfully pleading for God to end my pain, I stopped asking. I began examining the motive of my petition. If my heart were laid bare before you, you would've seen my intense desire to *use* God to advance *my* will. I didn't want to suffer! Slowly, I started making a different appeal: I asked God to show me all that He wanted me to learn from my suffering.

At that point, I was beginning to align myself with His purposes. The fact that God wasn't healing me indicated that it wasn't His timing. Though God took *no* delight in my suffering, He had better reasons for allowing it. It's never wise of me to advise God to follow through with my plan when His is far superior (though not necessarily easier). I should be thankful that God refuses my requests that feed my inclination to live independently of Him. Do I trust God enough to ask Him for whatever difficulty He deems best to keep me relying on Him?

Need and adversity are tools that God often uses to expose my depravity, inadequacy, and brokenness. They pave the path for greater dependency on Him. We raise our children to become independent, and rightfully so. But God raises His children to become dependent on Him because that's what is best for us.

I can cooperate with God and allow Him to lovingly use the scalpel to cut away at my arrogant pride and use the crucible to purify my motives, affections, and actions or I can choose to be bitter and angry and struggle on my own.

The tsunami pain episodes that have enveloped me have shown me that I am not strong enough to hold on, but they disclosed the strength of the Almighty who is holding onto me.

Suffering exposes my idols of control and comfort, which stunt my spiritual growth, and informs me of my need to embrace God's better purposes in life. It seems we rarely realize our desperate need for God without adversity!

Physical pain invites me to take a closer look at what's wrong in my body. But it can also usher me into the deep recesses of my mind and reveal my true beliefs and values. C.S. Lewis said, "God whispers to us in our pleasures, speaks in our conscience, but shouts in our pain: it is His megaphone to rouse a deaf world."[52]

Suffering has a way of peeling back the frivolous to help me focus on what matters. God uses the megaphone of pain and suffering in my life to show me my "not enoughness," weakness, and brokenness which subsequently reveal His sufficiency, strength, and wholeness.

As the ancient goldsmith's fire refined gold, so suffering brings my impurities to the surface. A goldsmith knows the process is over when he sees his reflection in the gold. God's goal is to see my character reflect His.

I talk with Tim, my kids, grandkids, and friends because I want to nurture these relationships. Where there is no communication, there is no relationship. The time I invest in something reveals how important it is to me.

I will converse with God to the degree that I love Him and believe what He has said about our time together. My purpose in spending time with God shouldn't only be to hand Him my grocery list of needs. I have a personal God who wants an intimate friendship with me, and I want that with Him!

God made me an eternal being and gave me an innate knowledge that there is something more to life than what I experience in the here and now. Life is like the steam rising from my whistling tea kettle, disappearing quickly. Should I spend these fleeting moments rehearsing my grievances or wallowing in my inabilities during this "dot" on an infinite timeline? Though this life may hold intense suffering, it's a mere drop in a limitless ocean. I have to remind myself often, *Kerri, hang in there; it's only a dot, a mere drop.*

As a redeemed child of God, suffering, pain, sorrow, grief, and death are only in this life! Experiencing God's goodness extends beyond the boundary time.

Paul, an apostle of Jesus, quoted from the ancient book of Isaiah, "What no eye has seen, what no ear has heard, and what no human mind has conceived — the things God has prepared for those who love him."[53]

I will have all eternity to experience fun and spectacular things in a perfect body. In light of what my eternal condition will be, my limitations here have mattered less and less.

In *The Message*, Eugene Peterson's idiomatic translation of the Bible, we read in 2 Corinthians 4:16-18: "We're not giving up. How could we! Even though on the outside, it often looks like things are falling apart on us; on the inside, where God is making new life, not a day goes by without his unfolding grace. These hard times are small potatoes compared to the coming good times; the lavish celebration prepared for us. There's far more here than meets the eye. The things we see now are here today, gone tomorrow. But the things we can't see now will last forever."

When I first started writing this memoir, I didn't think there would be an audience for a story without a happy ending. But I wasn't looking far enough down the road to realize that my story would eventually have a happy ending regardless.

In Joel 2:25, God says to Israel, "I will give you back what you lost in the years when swarms of locusts ate your crops." (Good News Translation). This promise and others like it, which God made to Israel, reveal His heart. God loves to restore! Someday, He is going to complete His plan and bring this earth back to His original intent.[54]

By His grace, God enables me to tough it out in this drop of existence that we call time. And for all eternity, I am promised the paradise of His presence, in the place He has been preparing for me, where I will never again be broken, but ***wholly whole.***

A PRAYER

Dear God,
　You are the Lord of the mist as well as the hail, the gentle breeze as well as the tornado. You are beyond us in every way. Though You exist outside of time and the scope of the universe, You're very near, personal, and compassionate. You collected my tears and recorded all my sorrows; not a single one has escaped You.
　You are the strength of my life, not a crutch; without Your enablement, I can't even lean on a crutch. You sustain me when I'm as good as dead. You are my life! Take what the enemy wants to use to destroy me to teach me of Your sufficient grace and demonstrate Your enduring mercy.
　I wouldn't have chosen this course; I despise pain! But because of my adversity, I know You more intimately. And hopefully, I'm better equipped to help others in their affliction.
　I believe what You say, that my sufferings are accomplishing an eternal good, a good that will somehow outweigh the adversity. Please draw me away from what seems good to my eyes and show me the better in Yours.
　Thank you for the readers of this book who are not yet trusting You. Assure them that they are better off trusting You in their darkness than trusting anyone or anything else. Help them find Your words trustworthy and believe them. Draw them to Yourself. Just as You grow the giant sequoia tree from a tiny seed, grow their bud of faith in You one day at a time. I long for them to know You personally and experience Your comfort. I pray that their anguish on this earth will be the only hell they ever know.
　Thank You for the readers that are Your disciples. Teach them that they can trust Your heart even when they can't understand what Your hand is allowing. You are not only able, but You long to fix their brokenness. You genuinely hate their pain. You have not necessarily promised to make sense of their tribulations; instead, You have promised to use them for the good because they love You. Oh, that my suffering brothers and sisters could be a billboard for the sufficiency of Your grace, pointing onlookers to their sustaining

Redeemer. Embolden them to believe that You won't waste their pain, that this process of refinement is worth it.

Please help us to accept our brokenness that You choose not to mend yet. Through our cracks, illuminate the darkness around us, allowing these broken jars of earthen clay to emanate Your splendor. Convince us that You can do more with our brokenness than with our strength!

You have spared some of Your followers from the mouths of lions, the swords of kings, fiery flames, enemy armies, and even death, bringing them back to life. Yet, others were not. They were imprisoned, flogged, persecuted, stoned, sawed in two, and living impoverished lives in caves and holes in the ground. Only You, sovereign LORD, who know the beginning from the end, are qualified to determine our way. We look to You, our Healer and Provider, to save us in Your time and in Your way.

Ultimately, this time of pain, struggle, and fear will be over, and we will experience healing in every way. You said that when we see You, we will be like You — wholly restored in every way! But even now, in our current broken bodies You see Your redeemed children in Christ: forgiven, spotless, lovely, and whole! Thank You for such an undeserved gift of kindness! Help us thank You with our lives.

In Jesus Name,
Amen

In Conclusion

For three decades, Tim lovingly listened to my ramblings and cared deeply, but there was no way he could empathize with the agony of my body and the wounds of my heart. The comfort and sympathy of others does help, but we can only receive empathy from someone who has been there. I suffered with SIJD for thirteen years before I met someone else with SIJD. We sat together in the waiting room of Dr. Lippitt's office in Georgia. How I wished that we would've had more time together because she had walked a mile in my shoes! After having this chronic condition for twenty years, I met a lady named Brenda, who lives just a half of a mile up the road from us. She endures chronic back pain and has had her SI joint fused as well. Immediately we struck up a friendship. Like me, she also had fallen down the stairs and needed to have her first fusion redone two more times. *Good grief!* Jody, my kindred-spirit friend of three decades, understands the confinement, loneliness, and huge frustration of unexplainable chronic pain. We have harmonized so well in this song of suffering because we have a shared love for Jesus. Friends in your neighborhood of pain that can relate are treasured gifts from God! I hope that by sharing my experiences of adversity with you, you won't feel as lonely. I hope you've found a friend in me.

I would be honored to listen to your story and pray for you. You may contact me by email at WholelyBroken@gmail.com.

Appendix

CHAPTER 3: Feelings Versus Truth

- Emotions are not the enemy. Imagine what a hollow life it would be without them. I can hardly bear living without peace and joy, yet I'd rather not experience anger or loneliness. Some emotions, like fear and anxiety, can be crippling. Stoics are so afraid of emotions that they go to great lengths to hide them. That's no way to live! Emotions are something to keep in check, but not bury.
- I have emotions because God does; I was made in His likeness. Rather than fear my emotions, I need to ask, "God, how do You want to use my emotions?" God tells me to "weep with those who weep" and "rejoice with those who rejoice." It can be a huge encouragement to enter into someone else's joy or sadness. God wants me to use my emotions to reflect Him and to serve others.
- Thoughts swirl around in my mind. Should they influence my feelings, or should my feelings influence my thoughts? Which should be in control, my mind or my heart? Society tells me to trust my feelings, to "listen to your heart." Is that wise? The Bible says my heart is deceitful.
- Doubt is destabilizing, apathy shuts me down, and fear paralyzes. I don't want to be arrested by worry. I yearn for peace in a crisis. What can I do? Appropriate the principles

of God's Word. It will change my thinking, which, in turn, helps my feelings. Working through all of this, I wrote the following on October 27, 1999.

1. My feelings may say, "You've been forsaken." Truth says God never left me and never will. (Hebrews 13:5)
2. My feelings may say, "God doesn't care." Truth says He cares for me more than I can imagine. (1 Peter 5:7)
3. My feelings may say, "It's hopeless." Truth says God keeps His promises. God has plans to give me hope and a future! (Jeremiah 29:11)
4. My feelings may say, "This darkness will never end." Truth says that weeping may endure for a night, but that joy comes in the morning. (Psalm 30:5) Better days are coming, if not here on this earth, then with Jesus.
5. My feelings may say, "God abandoned me." Truth says I am sealed with His Spirit. He lives in me. (Ephesians 1:13)
6. My feelings may say, "I don't have anything to give anyone." Truth says that I need to pray for others (James 5:16) and to think about how to encourage them (Hebrews 10:24-25).
7. My feelings may say, "I can't have what I want." Truth says I will have everything I need. (Philippians 4:19)
8. My feelings may say, "I need to complain." Truth says to give thanks in every situation. (1 Thessalonians 5:18)
9. My feelings may say, "This is not working out for good." Truth says that God is working this all together for my good and His glory. (Romans 8:28)
10. My feelings may say, "My life has no purpose." According to the book of Ecclesiastes, life is meaningless under the sun. But He who lives beyond the sun brings purpose and meaning to all of life! I am a work of the Divine Artisan, and He has prepared good things for me to carry out. (Ephesians 2:10) Because His mercy never ends, He will bring about all He intends for me. Why would He forsake the work of His hands? (Psalm 138:8)

CHAPTER 4: Flare-Up Instructions

- Always answer these two questions honestly: Can someone else do that? What should you cancel?
- Before taking medications, use the TENS unit. Always have extra batteries on hand.
- When you start narcotics, begin taking a laxative.
- When you begin a new medication, don't combine it with other medications. Don't take it lying down; beware of heart burn.
- Be aware of little-to-no sleep patterns that signal depression. Do you need to up the dosage of your antidepressant?
- When confined to bed, try to keep moving, even if it's just to contract and release muscles. Do a couple pelvic tilts. Even one is better than none.
- Eat tiny portions. Digestion slows when you're not on your feet.
- For prolonged pain, seek Lidocaine shots, pain patches, and steroids.
- When transitioning from bed to active moving, wear your brace, then wean off it slowly.
- In early recovery, increase walking by seconds not minutes. With recovery, "the slower you go, the faster you will get there."
- Try to keep moving as much as possible, but always listen to your body.
- When exercising, track repetitions and increase by one or two.
- Set tiny, achievable goals. Now is not the time to push yourself.
- Ease back into doing things that the pain pushed out.

CHAPTER 7: Advice to Self

- Suffering is not your choice, but your attitude is.
- Saying "no" to something you want to do now probably means saying "yes" to a hundred things you want to do later.
- Make exercise a part of your daily life.
- Not even this situation can separate you from God's love.

- Lower your expectations and you will lessen your disappointments.
- Don't succumb to self-pity; it threatens right thinking, maturity, and what independence remains.
- There is no timetable for a flare-up.
- Don't vacuum; it's always better for someone else to do it.
- Squat in order to lift things up with your legs.
- Don't ever pick up the grandkids.
- You have the health to do all that God has for you to do.
- You can't change your circumstances, but you can change your perspective.
- Anger that stems from your pain is a normal response to deep hurt.
- Don't anchor your joy onto something that is temporary, or you'll risk losing it.
- Believe your faithful God. He said that no matter what comes your way, He is allowing it for your good and His glory.
- What happens in your mind and heart can greatly help your ability to cope with the pain.
- Hold onto the handrail; you can't afford to fall down the stairs again.
- Do not ignore tightness, stiffness, fatigue, or discomfort. Give heed to your inner voice saying, "I don't feel so good."
- Remember: Because of Jesus, this is your only hell.
- Ask the better questions.
- Ask God "Why?" with an open hand not a closed fist.
- Don't deny your grief but mind your focus.
- You control what you let your mind dwell on.
- When your feelings are all over the map; don't let them rearrange your theology or dictate your doctrine.
- God is for you, not against you.
- Obedience to God, a good attitude, and a thankful heart rank higher in God's economy than your ability to function.
- Rest! Don't wear a TENS or take narcotics in order to push through the pain. If the pain is significant enough to take medication, then rest.

- Don't make healing your life's goal. Your ultimate calling is to make much of God.

CHAPTER 9: A Few Biblical Reasons for Suffering

- Suffering is a training tool which develops righteousness. (Hebrews 12:5-11)
- Suffering grows my dependence on God and weans me from self-reliance. (II Corinthians 1:9)
- Suffering leads me to repentance — if the suffering was caused by sin. (I Corinthians 11:29-30)
- Suffering can develop my capacity to sympathize with others. (II Corinthians 1:3-5)
- Suffering reveals my spiritual needs. (Psalm 119:67)
- Suffering develops humility. (II Corinthians 12:7)
- Suffering brings glory to God. (John 9:1-5)
- Suffering can be an evangelistic tool. (Philippians 1:12)
- Suffering is something God will use for my ultimate good if I love Him. (Romans 8:28-29)

Endnotes

CHAPTER 1

[1] Charles R. Swindoll, *LaughAgain* (Thomas Nelson, 1995).

[2] Helen Keller, https://www.azquotes.com/author/7843 Helen_Keller?p=10.

[3] Helen Keller, https://www.azquotes.com/quote/361420.

[4] Waren W. Wiersbe, *Looking Up When Life Gets You Down* (Baker Books, p. 53, 2012).

CHAPTER 2

[5] Illustration from Physician Partners of America from Google Pictures.

[6] Arthur W. Pink, *The Attributes of God*. (Baker Publishing Group, 1975).

CHAPTER 4

[7] Spine Health, https://www.spine-health.com/conditions/sacroiliac-joint-dysfunction/accurate-diagnosis-sacroiliac-joint-dysfunction (February 2018).

[8] My Health, https://myhealth.alberta.ca/Health/pages/conditions.aspx?hwid=tv8504& (November 2020).

CHAPTER 6

[9] C. S. Lewis, https://essentialcslewis.com/2019/05/01/csl-daily-05-01-19/.

[10] Dr. Paul Brand & Philip Yancey, *Pain, the Gift Nobody Wants* (New York, NY HarperCollins Publishers, Inc., page 187, 1997).

[11] Dr. Paul Brand & Philip Yancey, *Pain, the Gift Nobody Wants* (New York, NY HarperCollins publishers, Inc., page 223, 1997).

CHAPTER 7

[12] Laura Story, "Blessings" *Blessings*. INO Records, 2011.

CHAPTER 8

[13] Corrie Ten Boom, quotepark.com/quotes/1509182-corrie-ten-boom-worry-does-not-empty-tomorrow-of-its-sorrow-item/.

[14] Paul Tripp, https://www.paultripp.com/wednesdays-word/posts/the-trap-of-worry (April 2014).

CHAPTER 9

[15] Berean Bible Church, https://www.bereanbiblechurch.org/transcripts/topical/pain_is_providential.htm (March 2015).

[16] Job 1:11 New International Version of the Holy Bible, NIV.

[17] Job 1:20-22 NIV.

[18] Job 2:5 NIV.

[19] Job 16:15 NIV.

[20] Job 13:20-22 NIV.

[21] Ephesians 4:26 New American Standard Bible.

[22] Job 42:2-3 NIV.

[23] Corrie Ten Boon, *The Hiding Place* (Chosen Books, 1971).

[24] Matthew 22:37-39 NIV.

[25] Matthew 5:44 NIV.

[26] 1 Corinthians 13:4-7 NIV.

[27] Spurgeon, www.spurgeon.org/resource-library/blog-entries/6-quotes-spurgeon-didnt-say/.

CHAPTER 10

[28] Clara Boothe Luce, https://www.dialhope.org/no-hopeless-situations-2/December 23, 2014, (accessed 2022).

[29] N. J. Regenerative Institute, https://www.njregenerativeinstitute.com/services/lipogems, (accessed 2020).

[30] Ortho Info, https://orthoinfo.aaos.org/en/treatment/platelet-rich-plasma-prp, (October 2020).

[31] Corrie Ten Boom, https://www.guideposts.org/better-living/positive-living/guideposts-classics-corrie-ten-boom-forgiveness.

[32] John 9:3 NIV.

[33] From a podcast: https://nickvujicic.com/podcast-2/.

[34] From a podcast: https://nickvujicic.com/podcast-2/.

[35] The Gospel Coalition, https://www.thegospel coalition.org/article/reflections-on-50th-anniversary-of-my-diving-accident/ (accessed 2017).

[36] The Gospel Coalition, https://www.thegospel coalition.org/article/reflections-on-50th-Anniversary-of-My-Diving-Accident/ (accessed 2017).

[37] I Peter 2:23 NIV.

[38] Bill Johnson, https://melwild.wordpress.com/2014/09/20/bill-johnson-quotes/ (accessed 2022).

CHAPTER 11

[39] Revelation 7:9.

[40] Got Questions, https://www.gotquestions.org/God-is-truth.html.

[41] A. W. Tozer, https://www.criout.com/the-wrath-of-god-what-is-it-by-a-w-tozer/.

[42] John 14:6 NIV.

CHAPTER 12

[43] Dr. Paul Brand & Philip Yancey, *Pain, the Gift Nobody Wants*. (New York, NY HarperCollins Publishers, Inc.)

[44] Pain Health, https://painhealth.csse.uwa.edu.au/pain-module/neuroplasticity (July 2021).

[45] The Scientist, https://www.the-scientist.com/features/glial-ties-to-persistent-pain-30148 (January 2018).

[46] Melanie Themstrom, *The Pain Chronicles* (New York: Farrar, Straus & Giroux).

[47] Brain Works Neurotherapy, https://brainworks neurotherapy.com/what-neuroplasticity (accessed 2020).

48 Pain Science, https://www.painscience.com/articles/central-sensitization.php (November 2020).

49 Psalm 119:71.

50 Psalm 119: 67.

51 James 5:16.

52 Desiring God, https://www.desiringgod.org/articles/god-shouts-to-us-in-our-pain (2017).

53 1 Corinthians 2:9.

54 Revelations 21:1-5.

ABOUT THE AUTHOR

Kerri Shepherd and her husband, Tim, live and work in Pennsylvania at the Ethnos360 Wayumi Campus. Kerri loves teaching children God's Word at her local church and spending time with her grandchildren. Swimming and gardening are her two favorite hobbies.

Made in the USA
Columbia, SC
12 April 2023